WHEN
BLACK
PREACHERS
PREACH

OTHER BOOKS

by
Daniel Whyte III

- *LETTERS TO YOUNG BLACK MEN*

- *LETTERS TO YOUNG BLACK WOMEN*

- *MO' LETTERS TO YOUNG BLACK MEN*

- *WHEN BLACK PREACHERS PREACH, Volume I*,
  Editor

- *WHEN BLACK PREACHERS PREACH, Volume II*,
  Editor

- *MONEY UNDER THE CAR SEAT (AND OTHER THINGS TO THANK GOD FOR)*

- *7 THINGS YOUNG BLACK MEN DO TO MESS UP THEIR LIVES*

- *7 THINGS YOUNG BLACK WOMEN DO TO MESS UP THEIR LIVES*

- *GOD HAS SMILED ON ME: A TRIBUTE TO A BLACK FATHER WHO STAYED*

- *JUST JESUS!: THE GREATEST THINGS EVER SAID ABOUT THE GREATEST MAN WHO EVER LIVED*,
  Editor

WHEN BLACK PREACHERS PREACH

LEADING BLACK PREACHERS GIVE DIRECTION AND ENCOURAGEMENT TO A NATION THAT HAS LOST ITS WAY

Volume III

Edited and Compiled
by
Daniel Whyte III

WHEN BLACK PREACHERS PREACH, VOLUME III

Cover Designed by Bill Hopper of Hopper Graphics

Copyright 2007
TORCH LEGACY PUBLICATIONS, DALLAS, TEXAS;
ATLANTA, GEORGIA; BROOKLYN, NEW YORK

First Printing 2007

The Bible quotations in this volume are from the King James Version of the Bible.

The name TORCH LEGACY PUBLICATIONS and its logo are registered as a trademark in the U.S. patent office.

ISBN Number: 0-9763487-3-X

Printed in the U.S.A.

To

THE GLORY OF GOD

and to the

GLORY OF JESUS CHRIST OUR LORD

and

To the preachers, named and unnamed who continue to stedfastly preach *"Thus saith the Lord"* to a lost and dying nation. May the people who read these sermons take heed to the Word of the Lord, and may God raise up many more preachers who will preach it.

WHEN BLACK PREACHERS PREACH
VOLUME III

CONTENTS

ACKNOWLEDGEMENTS

I wish to thank the Lord for His mercy and grace, and for allowing me to do such a work as this. I also want to thank all of the preachers included in this volume for standing strong in these perilous times. I want to thank my wife, Meriqua Whyte for helping to proofread and edit this book; my children: Daniella Whyte for helping to proofread and edit this book; Daniel Whyte IV for typesetting this book and for also helping in the proofreading and editing process; and, Danita, Danae`, Daniqua, Danyel Ezekiel and Danyelle Elizabeth for doing a wonderful job typing up the manuscript. A special thank you goes to Bill Hopper of Hopper Graphics for creating the beautiful cover on this volume. May God bless you all.

WHEN BLACK PREACHERS PREACH
VOLUME I

INTRODUCTION

The idea and vision for such a book as this one has been in my heart for quite some time now.

In the not too distant past, God began to raise up a fresh and exciting voice in America. That voice is the voice of the black preacher who refused to use God's sacred desk as a stage for entertainment or as a platform for political causes. Rather, these God-sent black preachers chose to stand boldly and preach *"Thus saith the Lord"* without compromise, fear or favor. These preachers are not popular, but neither were the preachers in the Bible. No, these preachers may not be popular, but they certainly need to be heard.

This book basically has a three-fold purpose:

A. To bring glory and honor to God and to His Son Jesus Christ.
B. To show honor and appreciation for the older black Baptist preachers who have paid the price, and who have laid the foundation for those of us who have followed. (Of course, all of the older brethren could not be included in this volume, but my hope is that these who are included will represent them.)
C. To reach this generation of Americans, who seem to have lost their way.

The sermons included in this volume were selected based upon how long the minister had been faithfully preaching the Gospel and based upon the impact of the sermon when it was actually preached. You will notice that some of these sermons were stenographically recorded because we not only wanted to get the "letter of the sermon," but the "spirit of the sermon," as well; so that when you read this book, you will feel as though you are actually in the congregation, hearing the man of God, preach *"Thus saith the Lord."*

I believe that if you read each sermon and the "significant stuff" in the back of this book, and you **take heed to it,** you will be convicted, challenged, comforted, and changed.

—Daniel Whyte III
South Bend, Indiana

WHEN BLACK PREACHERS PREACH
VOLUME II

INTRODUCTION

The first volume of *When Black Preachers Preach* is dedicated to the honor and appreciation of the older black Bible-believing preachers who have laid the foundation for correct and clear Bible preaching and teaching in the black community of America. Well, this present offering — *When Black Preachers Preach, Volume II*, highlights some of the most dynamic preachers of our present day. Some of the men included in this volume are pastoring some of the fastest growing Bible-believing churches in America. Also, some of these preachers head up exciting, evangelistic organizations and conferences aimed at reaching black America with the unadulterated gospel of Jesus Christ.

These men of God have broken the mold of the traditional black preacher. They have broken away from tradition itself. These men have forsaken the old way of doing black church, and they have chosen to stay clear of the religious confusion that has engulfed black America. These are men who do not claim perfection, but who are being mightily used by God.

As I approach my closing of this introduction to the second volume, allow me to state the four-fold purpose as to why we publish these down-to-earth messages from Heaven:

1. First and foremost to glorify God and our Saviour Jesus Christ.

2. Black America, white America, and whosoever will needs to hear these messages from the Word of God. These are messages that should not be preached into the air and then forgotten.

3. Posterity. Friend of mine, we do not publish these books to make us feel good about ourselves, or for our own personal enjoyment. If the Lord should tarry His coming, I want these books to be available for the generations that will follow. They will need to know that there was a remnant of black preachers who stood for God in these times.

4. And, as we said in the first volume, to reach this generation of Americans, who seem to have lost their way.

If you are one of the few dear people who still love what God calls "sound doctrine"; if you love powerful and exciting preaching that is also biblical, then the book that you hold in your hands is the right book for you.

May God use this book to change your life forever, and usher in many children of slaves into God's glorious Kingdom.

—Daniel Whyte III
Irving, Texas

WHEN BLACK PREACHERS PREACH
VOLUME III

INTRODUCTION

In the introduction to *When Black Preachers Preach, Volume II*, I stated that one of the reasons why we publish these straightforward, down-to-earth messages from Bible-believing black preachers is for posterity. I stated that because it seems as though the black preacher, who preaches the Word of God as the Final Authority on every aspect of life, is quickly disappearing from the landscape of Black America; and soon those who will not take heed to the "sound doctrine" that is being preached will be left in the darkness of the religious confusion and false doctrine that is engulfing the African-American community. Now, I am not saying that there aren't any young black preachers who will preach the Word of the Lord to the next generation; but I will say that their tribe is getting smaller.

So, here are three reasons why we are publishing this third volume of messages from men of God who preach *"Thus saith the Lord"*:

1. For the glory of God and our Saviour Jesus Christ.

2. In honor and appreciation of the black preachers who continue to preach "A Sure Word of Prophecy" to a lost and dying world, that desperately needs to hear the truth of the Gospel and see the Light of Salvation.

3. Because the next generation of Americans will need to know that there was a remnant of black preachers who stood up for God, stood down the devil, and preached the Words of the One Who died for us.

From the messages contained in this book, may the Word of the Lord continuously resound in the ears of those who read them, and may God raise up many more black preachers who will preach the Book, the Blood, and the Blessed Hope.

—Daniel Whyte III
Irving, Texas

TO THE PREACHERS INCLUDED IN THIS, AND PREVIOUS VOLUMES, AND TO ALL THOSE WHO PREACH "THUS SAITH THE LORD":

"I charge thee therefore before God, and the Lord Jesus Christ, who shall judge the quick and the dead at his appearing and his kingdom; Preach the word; be instant in season, out of season; reprove, rebuke, exhort with all longsuffering and doctrine. For the time will come when they will not endure sound doctrine; but after their own lusts shall they heap to themselves teachers, having itching ears; And they shall turn away their ears from the truth, and shall be turned unto fables. But watch thou in all things, endure afflictions, do the work of an evangelist, make full proof of thy ministry."

—II Timothy 4:1-5

THE WRATH OF GOD

Pastor Robert Anderson Jr.

Rev. Robert Anderson is pastor of the Colonial Baptist Church in Randallstown, Maryland.

Romans Chapter One

I remember a great preacher once saying that the job of the preacher is two-fold: "to comfort the afflicted, and to afflict the comforted." Most messages today are designed to bring comfort and encouragement, but fewer and fewer messages are designed to cut with deep conviction those who are "comfortable"! In our day of Pseudo-peace and prosperity, bad news is quickly dismantled. However, just as the mailman delivers the mail as he received it, so must we. Oftentimes, the mailman brings good news, but other times, the messages are sad and even terrifying.

Speaking about the wrath of God is not a very comforting thing. In fact, it is rather disturbing, and rightly so. The Apostle Paul states plainly, *"For the wrath of God is revealed from heaven against all ungodliness and unrighteousness of men, who hold the truth in unrighteousness"* (Romans 1:18).

Paul was a faithful preacher who declared all the word of God. He says, *"For I have not shunned to declare unto you all the counsel of God"* (Acts 20:27). While Paul preached unflinchingly the Gospel of Christ, he also preached about the wrath of God being revealed upon men.

THE WRATH OF GOD DISTINGUISHED

Paul begins verse eighteen with the word "for" which is a vital word that connects this verse with two preceding verses. Paul states in verses 16 and 17 that he is not ashamed of the Gospel because it is the power of God. The Gospel is the death, burial, and resurrection of the Lord Jesus Christ for us. However, the point of verse eighteen is that the Gospel is necessary because there is such a thing as the *wrath of God*. Thus, it is this preacher's observation that the whole weight of verses sixteen and seventeen rest on the truth that all men are under the awesome wrath of God. Apart from this biblical fact, there is no need for the Gospel.

Therefore, the reality of the wrath of God provides the essential foundation for the Gospel.

THE WRATH OF GOD DENIED

In the New Testament there are two primary words for "wrath" which are oftentimes used interchangeably: the first is: *Thumos*— this word refers to the hot and vehement surge of wrath or ferocious outrage. This is not the word used in this passage. The second one is: *Orgos* — this word refers to the slow but deliberate rise of deep indignation. This is the word used in verse eighteen.

God does not have, nor does He display, uncontrollable wrath. His anger is very calculated and deliberate. One could say then, that the wrath of God is that disposition of God which stands opposed to man's disobedience to divine revelation, and responds with calculated and deliberate punishment against the sinner.

THE WRATH OF GOD DETERMINED

The wrath of God can be observed in three distinct phases, namely: past, present and future.

First, the wrath of God *past* points back to Golgotha. It was there that God the Father unleashed all of His divine wrath against us, upon God the Son — the Lord Jesus Christ. The Bible says, *"Who his own self bore our sins in his own body on the tree, that we, being dead to sins, should live unto righteousness: by whose stripes ye were healed"* (I Peter 2:24).

The Bible declares that we all are sinners in Romans 3:23, and that the wages of sin is eternal death in Romans 6:23. Thus, Christ willingly came to take the wrath of God against us unto Himself. Isaiah states, *"But he was wounded for our transgressions, he was bruised for our iniquities: the chastisement of our peace was upon him; and with his stripes we were healed. All we like sheep have gone astray; we have turned every one to his own way; and the Lord hath laid on him the iniquity of us all"* (Isaiah 53:5, 6).

Thus, the wrath of God intended for us was given to Jesus Christ— the spotless Lamb of God.

Second, the wrath of God *present* is displayed today before our very eyes. The verb "reveal" is better translated "is being revealed," because of its present tense. Right now, the wrath of God is being revealed through the results of God giving sinners over to their dark and sinful passions. Please note the following verses:

Romans 1:24: *"Wherefore God also gave them up to uncleanness through the lusts of their own hearts."*

Romans 1:26: *"For this cause God gave them up unto vile affections."*

Romans 1:28: *"God gave them over to a reprobate mind."*

25

Today, God's wrath is seen, for example, through AIDS, because God is giving homosexuals over to their vile lusts of unnatural affections. Also, God's wrath can be seen in the destruction of our society through drug abuse, sexual abuse, mass murders, high suicides, etc.

In fact, the Bible states that, *"He that believeth on the Son hath everlasting life: and he that believeth not the Son shall not see life; but the wrath of God abideth on him"* (John 3:36).

Third, the wrath of God is set for the *future*. The Bible speaks extensively about God's future wrath. *"For there shall be great tribulation, such as was not since the beginning of the world to this time, no, nor ever shall be"* (Matthew 24:21). *"And to wait for His Son from heaven, whom He raised from the dead, that is Jesus, who delivers us from the wrath to come"* (I Thessalonians 1:10).

There are many other Scriptures which speak of the "tribulation" to come upon the earth, and the ultimate act of God's wrath seen in the lake of fire. No prophet spoke of hell more than the Lord Jesus Christ (cf. Matthew 5:22, 29; 10:28; 11:23; 16:18; 18:9; 23:15, 33).

Hell and the lake of fire is the future for all who reject Jesus Christ as their personal Saviour. As for the believer, he will not face the tribulation (that is all those who accept Christ before the Tribulation) or the lake of fire, for Christ has taken our hell and paid the price for our redemption (cf. Romans 8.1). However, each believer will stand before the Judgment Seat of Christ and will be held accountable before God for the deeds he has done in the body both good and bad (cf. II Corinthians 5:10).

WHY I STILL BELIEVE IN SOUL-WINNING

Dr. Tommy Steele

Dr. Tommy Steele is the pastor of the New Life Baptist Church in Concord, North Carolina.

"And Jesus came and spake unto them, saying, All power is given unto me in heaven and in earth. Go ye therefore, and teach all nations, baptizing them in the name of the Father, and of the Son, and of the Holy Ghost: Teaching them to observe all things whatsoever I have commanded you: and, lo, I am with you alway, even unto the end of the world. Amen."

—Matthew 28:18-20

Tonight, I want to speak on the subject, *"Why I Still Believe In Soul-Winning."* I still believe in soul-winning in a day when soul-winning preachers are few and far between; when soul-winning churches are few and far between. I believe Acts 4:13 when it says, *"Now when they saw the boldness of Peter and John, and perceived that they were unlearned and ignorant men, they marvelled; and they took knowledge of them, that they had been with Jesus."* How did they know that they had been with Jesus? Because they talked about Him a lot.

Listen, they said these folks were *"unlearned and ignorant men"*. Why? Because they talked about the Son of God. When I walk down the golden streets of glory, we'll know as much as they claim to know. The thing between us is that we will have a band of sinners walking behind us, that have been saved by the marvelous blood of

27

Christ, just like Peter and John.

I still believe in soul-winning in a day when Baptist churches are falling into "Lifestyle Evangelism." I still believe in soul-winning in a day when the church of the living God is going to be purged. Because Jesus said, 'every branch in Me that beareth fruit shall be purged.' Every soul-winner is going to be purged. Every church is going to be purged. Every preacher is going to be purged. Every bus-captian is going to be purged. In a day when churches are being purged, I still believe in soul-winning.

I still believe that the answer to lost humanity is soul-winning in our churches. I'm going to give you six reasons why I still believe in soul-winning.

Thank God tonight for soul-winning bus captains. Thank God tonight for soul-winning Sunday School teachers. Thank God tonight for soul-winning mothers that take a stand for the Lord Jesus Christ. Thank God tonight for soul-winning daddies who are not afraid to get that old King James Bible and tell boys and girls how to be saved by the grace of God. Thank God for a soul-winning son, who's not afraid to get out there on Tuesday nights and take the Bible and walk down the streets of Charlotte and Concord, and let folks know that there's a Saviour on high and He can still save from the pits of hell! He's still in the saving business. Thank God for soul-winning sons. Thank God for soul-winning daughters.

JESUS SAID TO DO IT

The first reason why I believe in soul-winning is because **Jesus said to do it.** In Mark 16:15 we read, *"And he said unto them, Go ye into all the world and preach the gospel to every creature."* But you say it doesn't work. But He still says to do it.

28

Amen? But you say we don't have any professions. But He still says to do it. But you say nobody is coming to our church. But Jesus still says to do it.

I don't care if anyone ever comes to our church. I don't care if anyone is ever added to our church membership. He still says to do it. But you say nobody's getting saved. But Jesus still says to go soul-winning. I'm telling you, my friend, that if nobody is excited about keeping sinners out of hell, and no preacher cares about soul-winning, I still believe in soul-winning. Jesus said to do it. I don't care who preaches about it or who gets excited about it, He still says to do it.

You say, Preacher, where are they all? You can make all the excuses you want, He still says, 'go keep them out of hell.' But you say, we're not getting any numbers. I'm not in the numbers business. I'm in the keeping out of hell business. He still says to do it. And the first reason we ought to go soul-winning is because Jesus said so.

Every once in a while someone will say, well where are they all? Where are they? Let me show you something about that. Jesus knew those Pharisee-like people were going to come to New Life Baptist Church one day and they were going to say, Where are they all? I hear about so-and-so getting saved. Where are they all? Let's see what Jesus said about it.

In Luke 17:11-17, Jesus healed how many lepers? How many came back? What happened to the rest of them? Because they didn't come back doesn't mean they didn't get healed. Only one came back but Jesus said he healed ten. What I am trying to get you to see tonight is this—it may be but one that comes back, but it doesn't mean that they didn't all get saved. They were not thankful for what Jesus did for them. It is just like some of you. The reason you don't come back on Sunday night is because you're not thankful for what He has done for you. The reason you don't come back on Wednesday night is because you're not thankful for what He has done for you. The reason you don't come for soul-winning is because you are not thankful for what Jesus has done for you. But bless God, I guarantee you, that one who came back, I bet he was in service that day!

Where are they all? It doesn't really matter whether they come back or not. He still says to do it. Amen! The thing I can praise God for, is the one that came back. He changed the services that day. Folks are still saying, Where are they? I'll tell you where they are. They're just as saved as you are. Brother, let me tell you something. Jesus said, I healed ten and only one came back. The next time someone tries to criticize you by saying, I hear all these folks are getting saved, well, where are they all? Tell them, it's better than your zero.

Some of you critics in here, all you do is sit around and criticize. I'll come in on Wednesday night and tell you how many got saved. You'll say in your minds, Well, where are they all? Bless God, it's more than your zero. If you are not keeping sinners out of Hell, you have nothing to talk about. If Jesus got one out of ten, I'm in pretty good shape. Amen. This one was thankful. It may be only one to come back—like the lady who got saved and came this morning. But praise God for that one. Amen.

The first reason why we ought to go soul-winning is because Jesus said to do it. Don't know about you, but I don't want to belong in a fish aquarium. I want to belong to a New Testament Baptist Church that's keeping sinners out of hell. You say, preacher, what do you mean a "fish aquarium"?

(1) *The water is still.* What do you mean the water is still? Nobody's getting saved. That water that we put in that baptistry, after we keep sinners out of hell, we need to baptize them in the name of the Father, the Son and the Holy Ghost. And if the waters are still, you're in a fish aquarium.

(2) All the fish are *transported from another aquarium.* Folks try to criticize me all the time. This afternoon, a preacher called and said, "Where is Rev. Steele?" I said, "I'm here." He said, "You're the one." I said, "Yes Sir." "So you're the one." You know I can read his mind—"You're the one that's been stealing our church members. You're the one." They may have belonged to a church but they didn't belong to the church of Jesus Christ—the blood-washed crowd. When we found them they were lost and on the road to hell and brother, you can't steal a goat. But thank God, they're now saved and set apart—sheep that belong to the Lord Jesus.

All the rest of them are transplants. Do you know what I like about New Life Baptist Church? We have some folks here that were members of another church that came and joined and I thank God for them, but ninety percent of the people here, we won on the streets. I'm for people transferring, coming and joining our church, who are already saved. But we can't depend upon transfers. Let's go out there and keep moving. Amen. If the waters are not moving and all you have are transfers, you're in a fish aquarium.

(3) *Artificial Power Source.* A fish aquarium does not have the natural power to keep it going. It has an artificial power. There is more power in a soul-winning preaching church that's keeping sinners out of Hell than there is in ten thousand compromising fish aquariums that get up and please the people. Brother, let me tell you something, thank God for an old-fashioned New Testament Church that keeps

31

sinners out of hell. I don't want a fish aquarium. I want the real thing.

(4) Have you noticed that *overfeeding* makes a mess? I've stepped into some of these fish aquariums and opened that King James Bible and went to preaching. Before you know it somebody's sitting like this...And you see them leaning—Who does he think he is? He ain't God. Boy, they're mad about that. Overfeeding makes a mess. Bless God, there's more excitement in an old-fashioned, hell-fire, preaching church that tells people what they are, and preaches God's Book like It is, than ten thousand of those fish aquariums.

SOUL-WINNING KEEPS SINNERS OUT OF HELL

The second reason why I still believe in soul-winning is because **soul-winning keeps sinners out of hell.** I wish I could stand before people and tell them there is no hell. Luke chapter 16 is just a parable. I wish I could tell you that, and soothe your conscience and make you feel good. But, my friend, I'm here to tell you that there is a literal hell, and soul-winning keeps sinners out of hell.

Even you were going to hell. You were right at the edge of the cliff. But do you know what got you out of hell? A bus captain knocking on your door, taking people to the House of God. You got born again! Snatched out of hell! All I'm saying is, do you realize that when you go soul-winning, and take the Gospel story to somebody's Daddy, somebody's Momma, somebody's Sister, somebody's Brother, somebody's Uncle, somebody's Aunt, you're preventing them from going to hell!

Soul-winning keeps them out of hell! Now how can you sit at home on Tuesday night's on your big comfy couch? If I were home on Tuesday nights, I'd be turning around. I couldn't rest. I'd be under so much conviction because I'm not out there trying to keep somebody out of hell. Somebody loved me enough to give me the Gospel story. Somebody told me how to get out of hell. The decent thing for me to do is to take the Gospel to a lost and dying world and keep somebody out of hell. I'm saying soul-winning keeps sinners out of hell.

SOUL-WINNING CHANGES THE ATMOSPHERE

The third reason why I still believe in soul-winning is because **soul-winning changes the atmosphere of the church.** Can you imagine what this church would be like if nobody went soul-winning. Son, we'd be fighting each other all the time. I would have blackened Bro. Gary's eye. We'd be fighting like cats and dogs all the time. All we'd see, week after week, is the same faces; never new faces. (I've seen your face last week. I don't like the way you look. I don't like the way Bro. Terry looks, of course, but...) We'd be at each other all the time.

The thing that keeps me excited, the thing that keeps this church excited and keeps this church shouting and praising God is, we look down these aisles, and week after week, see sinners come that have been saved in their homes, sinners come and get saved at the altar. They stop and say, like old Tyrone did a few nights ago, I got saved and went to church the next day, and told the folks at school I got born again. He came Wednesday night and said, Preacher, I want to get baptized on Sunday. I tell you there's nothing like soul-winning. It changes the atmosphere in the church.

I've preached in some churches that didn't believe in soul-winning. I preached at Chapel Hill year before last. They didn't know anything about soul-winning. But I handled that thing for one solid week. On Saturday that crowd got together and said, 'We're going soul-winning.' Boy, they were excited. They said, "Preacher, we had three people to ask Jesus to save them." There is nothing that can change the atmosphere in a church like soul-winning can. Amen.

Let me tell you something. Sometimes on Tuesday night don't tell the devil how you feel. When you get off work, don't walk around the house and say, "Boy, I sure do have a headache. Boy, I sure am tired. Boy, I tell you what, my back is really tired." Don't say anything. Because if you say, I have a headache, that devil will take that hammer and bang! Your head will seem like it's bopping on both sides. Your back will get worse. You'll be hurting and aching all over. But let 9 o'clock or 9:30 pass by, you'll be feeling better. "Yeah, I'm alright. I'm going to work tomorrow. Yeah, I'll be there." "I heard you were sick." "Yeah, I was sick for a few hours, but I'm feeling better." Am I telling the truth?

Sometimes I have a headache. Sometimes I am just physically drained and I'm tired. I'm just slapped out from ripping and running. But when Tuesday night comes, I get up and get a bath, put on my clothes, get my New Testament in my suit and get on out of the house and get on that old bus. Going down the road we're all singing about Heaven and before you know it, I'm shouting and praising God amidst the headache. Before you know it, we're out knocking on doors, telling the Gospel story, and just on this past Tuesday night, winning that lost lady to the Lord. Buddy, when I left her, I was shouting and praising God. Because nothing can make you more excited than soul-winning.

Do you know why some of you are deadheads? You don't go soul-winning. I can tell a difference in this crowd on Wednesday nights when you go soul-winning. You'll come in with a spring in your step. "What do you have tonight, preacher? We are ready to eat." You'll be ready. But boy, when you don't go soul-winning, you'll come in on Wednesday night about 7:45, sit in your seat like this... "Let's stand and sing." You'll get up, get your hymn book, look at the words then sing like you've been sitting still. Amen? Next you'll be looking around asking, "What page they said it was on?" I mean, just don't have any life about it at all.

But you get on that bus on Tuesday night and then come to church. Even if you didn't see anybody get saved, your bait is out. You'll come in with wings on Wednesday night. You'll grab that hymn book and you'll turn to that page with a smile on your face, and you'll shout it. Why would you shout it? Because soul-winning makes a difference. If we don't want to lose the excitement in our church, we just have to keep soul-winning.

IT CAUSES MEN TO GIVE THEIR LIVES TO PREACHING

The fourth reason why I still believe in soul-winning is because **it causes men to give their lives to preaching.** Psalm 126:5 says, *"They that sow in tears shall reap in joy."* You say, Preacher, I don't have a burden, that's why I don't go. Let me show you Psalm 126:5-6: *"They that sow in tears shall reap in joy. He that goeth forth and weepeth, bearing precious seed, shall doubtless come again with rejoicing, bringing in his sheaves with him."* If there's no going, there will be no weeping.

You're not going to weep until you see where they live. You're not going to care until you see what they go through. Bus captain, you're not going to visit with a broken-heart until you see what the mamas and daddies have to go through. You have to go before there is weeping. You can stay here in church all you want to and say, I'm going to weep for sinners. Oh no, sir. No, sir. You have to go.

Soul-winning causes men to give their lives to preaching. When I first got saved and started soul-winning, it seemed like week after week after week, God allowed me to see people get saved. I'd be so stirred up. The guys on the job said, "Steele, I believe God gave you the gift of soul-winning." I'd say, "Man, soul-winning is not a gift. It's a command. If you have a mouth and a New Testament you can do it too." There was something inside my soul, when I got to seeing people—lost, no God, no hope, going to religious churches and going through all those creeds, following the preacher, but on the road to hell. God broke my heart and said, 'Son, somebody has to win them to Christ. Somebody has to open their mouth and tell them about Jesus and teach them the Word of Christ.' I said, "O God, here am I. Send me." It causes men to give their lives to preaching.

IT UPSETS THE DEVIL

The fifth reason why I still believe in soul-winning is because **it upsets the devil.** Brother, battles have never been so hard as they are now. But let me tell you something, it's never been more exciting than it is right now. When I see the devil getting all upset and bent out of shape, I say, hallelujah! He has no business being calm with God's troublemakers. We're God's troublemakers. When I see Satan attack this church, when I see buses tear down, when I see finances drop and people rob God of his tithes and offerings, that just makes me want to serve God much more. I say, "you smutty face, I'm not leaving the church. It's God's church. I'm going to keep on keeping sinners out of hell. I don't care what you do, I don't care what you say. I'm still going to tell them about Jesus. Soul-winning upsets the devil."

You soul-winners know what I'm talking about. Have you ever been to a house before? Knock, knock. "My name is Pastor Steele from New Life Baptist Church. Do you folks attend church anywhere?" "No, sir, we sure don't." "Let me ask you a question, if you died right now, would you go to heaven? Are you one hundred percent sure about that?" Ring, Ring. "Hold a minute. I have to get this." I stood at a door in Concord. A lady had her little baby in her arms. That baby was as calm as could be. We stood at the front door and I had my New Testament out. I was showing her how to be saved. The phone rang. Somebody started screaming in the back room. That baby looked like somebody pinched him. He screamed at the top of his lungs. That baby screamed and screamed. She said, "Hold a minute, preacher, let me give him a bottle." He did not want any bottle. He threw that bottle down. He just screamed and screamed. Old Satan wanted to stop me. But I wouldn't move. I said, you do what you have to do, I'm going to keep telling you the Gospel story. And she kept doing this and that. I just kept telling the Gospel story. The devil was upset. And he ought to be upset about soul-winners. But I just kept telling her. And just as soon as she accepted Christ that baby stopped. What was it? Soul-winning upsets the devil.

If you're a soul-winner, you know it's going to happen. Listen, your car is going to blow up on you. Your refrigerator is going to blow up on you. Why? Because the devil is mad at you. But God can give you another car. God can give you another refrigerator. Soul-winning upsets the devil.

IT REACHES THE NEXT GENERATION

The sixth reason why I still believe in soul-winning is because **it reaches the next generation.** Listen, they criticize me, "Old Steele ain't got nothing but a bunch of buses full of poor kids." Say what you want to say, because do you know what we are doing? We are reaching the next generation.

Listen to this one (God threw in this one)—Pharaoh said to kill all the baby boys two years old and younger. Moses' mama said, "I'm not doing it. I'm putting my baby in a basket on the Nile River." Pharaoh's daughter picked him up, "O, what a beautiful baby." They didn't realize that that baby was the one who was going to lead a whole nation across the Red Sea and perform all kinds of miracles. He was going to be the one to kill a whole Egyptian army. "He's so beautiful. Looks like a Hebrew to me. A Hebrew bus child. Send him back to his mama. Let them raise him."

Even though Moses grew up with Pharoah's daughter, he chose rather to suffer affliction with the people of God rather than to enjoy the pleasures of Egypt. With a burden on his shoulders he led two and a half million people across the Red Sea.

You don't know who's riding your bus, bus captain. You don't know what girl or boy you're reaching for the next generation. He or she may turn this thing all the way around. I'm saying, it took one man filled with the Spirit of God to deliver a whole nation. Amen. It reaches the next generation. We've got to keep winning souls. It reaches the next generation.

"The fruit of the righteous is a tree of life; and he that winneth souls is wise."
—Proverbs 11:30

HOW TO REJOICE IN SUFFERING

Rev. Foster Covington

Rev. Foster Covington is the pastor of Victory Baptist Church in Roanoke, Virginia

I Peter 1:1-9

First Peter is a tremendous book that every believer should study, especially when going through a time of suffering. The encouragement Peter offered to his readers can speak to the heart of believers today if they are willing to trust and obey the Word of God.

Peter's first letter is addressed to the five Roman provinces in Asia Minor. Many from these provinces had heard this message at Pentecost (Acts 2:9) and had been spiritual converts. Paul had labored some in Asia, but was forbidden by the Holy Spirit to work intensively there.

This letter was written on occasion of the persecution of the believers in the five Roman provinces. Not an empire-wide persecution, but local persecutions that could be quite severe. The key concerns of Peter in this letter were for the preparation for suffering in the life of the believer, and for the believer to avoid suffering as an evil doer.

History tells us that Nero persecuted Christians in AD 54-68, Dominion in AD 81-96, and Trijan in AD 98-117. Since I Peter was written around AD 60 it could have well been addressed to those Christians under the Neronian persecution. But since the time of Christ's death, Christians have always been persecuted, starting with the Jewish Court of the Sanhedrin. It was this group of leaders who sent Paul, who was then called Saul, out with a letter of authority to squash this new sect of Judaism. The Romans were quick to join them as they realized that the Christian life was incompatible with paganism, so Christianity had to be stopped.

The truth of this letter is meaningful and just as valuable to Christians today as it was then.

THE ELECT ACCORDING TO THE FOREKNOWLEDGE

"Peter, an apostle of Jesus Christ, to the strangers scattered throughout Pontus, Galatia, Cappadocia, Asia, and Bithynia, Elect according to the foreknowledge of God the Father through santification of the Spirit, unto obedience and sprinkling of the blood of Jesus Christ: Grace unto you and peace, be multiplied."

—1 Peter 1:1-2

As we begin with the salutation (verses one and two) Peter identifies himself as the writer. He writes to the "strangers" who are scattered in the provinces. They were not strangers to Peter, but temporary residents in the areas he names. Their real citizenship was in Heaven as Philippians 3:20 states: *"For our conversation is in Heaven from whence also we look for the Saviour, the Lord Jesus Christ."* They were refugees suffering loss and deprivation. They must have had many questions on their minds, about the why of their suffering. Is that not what we say when we suffer? "Why me, Lord?"

Not only were they "strangers," they were the *"Elect according to the foreknowledge of God the Father."* In the midst of discouragement and doubt it helps the believer to remember *that God has chosen him.* This suffering then will be a blessing. Romans

8:28 says, *"And we know that all things work together for good to them that love God, to them who are the called according to his purpose."* The God who chose you is still in control. God had already planned before time to appoint that man could come to Him by way of the cross, through faith and holiness that would be worked in man by the Holy Spirit of God. This same God could be trusted to sustain them in their time of suffering.

THROUGH SANCTIFICATION OF THE SPIRIT TO OBEDIENCE

In the statement *"through santification of the Spirit unto obedience,"* Peter blends the themes of God's purpose with His insistence upon personal responsibility. Man in his free will can sin against God, but God in his foreknowledge knows who they are before they are ever born. Those who will repent are chosen through sanctification of the Spirit, but they are not changed until they obey the Spirit of God, repent of their sin, and confess the Lord Jesus as Saviour and Lord. In the midst of the congregation of the righteous, the spirit of God moves, and only the hard-hearted are not affected. Those who are moved by the Holy Spirit but do not repent of sin and confess the Lord Jesus as Saviour, will leave the congregation changed, but not saved.

Several years ago I witnessed to a very prosperous business man who had been invited to the church by his children. He had come on several occasions, so, we invited him to dinner. During the course of the evening, I had the opportunity to witness to him, but sadly he rejected salvation. He made a comment to me that I have not forgotten: "When I first came I did not believe a word you said. But after coming several times, I know that what you are saying is true. If, however, I do what you are asking, it will turn my world upside down. Don't lose hope, I'm not the same man you first met." He had been affected by the Spirit's message, but not unto obedience.

SPRINKLING OF THE BLOOD

This man that I witnessed to would not accept the *"sprinkling of the blood."* This *"sprinkling of the blood"* reminds the readers of the Passover. If the blood was not struck over the door post and the mantel, then the first born of each household died. There were no exceptions among men or animals. There was a death at every house—it was the firstborn who died—it was the first born, or the lamb. The judgment of God will come upon every soul. *"The soul that sinneth it shall die."* The only provision for deliverance from the wrath of God is the blood of Jesus Christ.

The Apostle Peter ends the salutation with encouragement: *"Grace be unto you, and peace, be multiplied."* We see the inclusion of reverence to all three persons of the Trinity. All the power of heaven is available to help the *"Elect"* of God.

A LIVING HOPE

"Blessed be the God and the Father of our Lord Jesus Christ, which according to his abundant mercy hath begotten us again unto a lively hope by the resurrection of Jesus Christ from the dead."

—I Peter 1:3

Having established who the people are that he is writing to (the "elect"), he speaks in verse three of their hope. He calls it a 'living hope' in the midst of suffering. The "elect" have this hope because of the "abundant mercy" of God. Lamentations 3:22 says, *"It is of the Lord's mercies that we are not consumed, because his compassions fail not..."* In addition to his mercy there is the knowledge of being begotten in this living hope *"by the resurrection of Jesus Christ from the dead."* The word used here is *anagennah'oto* which means to bring forth again, to regenerate. In fact, the source of our hope is in the death, burial, and resurrection of Jesus Christ. He foretold of His death and resurrection in the Gospels. Paul speaks clearly in Romans of this hope in Christ: *"like as Christ was raised up from the dead by the glory of the Father, even so we also should walk in newness of life"* (Romans 6:4). Why? Because *"...we shall be also in the likeness of his resurrection"* (Romans 6:4).

THE INHERITANCE

"To an inheritance incorruptible, and undefiled, and that fadeth not away, reserved in heaven for you."
—I Peter 1:4

This hope gives assurance of an inheritance and Peter is stressing here that God gives an inheritance that is sure. When you are a refugee, you need some assurance of an inheritance. Verse four assures them of an inheritance that is incorruptible. The people of Rwanda fled their homeland because they had no assurance of their inheritance. The corruption in their own hearts made them unwilling to trust the new government. There was no assurance of their inheritance, and they were willing to die in a refugee camp, rather than take a chance and go back to their own land. God gives an inheritance that is **incorruptible**. It is **undefiled** because its origin is not from man—he has nothing to do with it. It is **unfading** because man has nothing to do with preserving it. It is **secure** because it is kept in heaven. No amount of suffering experienced in this life will affect your reservation. Don't be fooled by Satan, folks, into trying his method of problem solving. Your inheritance is secure.

A SURE PROMISE

"Who are kept by the power of God through faith unto salvation ready to be revealed in the last time."
—I Peter 1:5

God gives a promise that is sure. In verse five, Peter lets them know that God will keep them, and I tell you now my friend, He will also keep you. Now, they could feel sure about their inheritance, but can something happen to the heir, that would cause him not to enter into his inheritance? Before we answer this question let's ask another. Why would God promise what He could not deliver? The answer is, He would not. Therefore there is nothing that will keep the "elect" of God from entering into their inheritance. The heir is kept by grace through faith. And the hope of this inheritance should sustain persecuted suffering Christians.

It is not by our power that we have an inheritance, nor are we saved by our power. Ephesians 2:8; *"For by grace are ye saved through faith, and that not of yourselves it is the gift of God."* Man does not even believe by his own power. I Corinthians 12:3 says, *"... no man can say Jesus is Lord, but by the Holy Ghost."* Therefore we must believe Romans 11:29, *"For the gifts and calling of God are without repentance..."* The faith that causes grace to work in the life of a true believer that he might persevere until the end, will last until the end. Once the believer has this fact set in his mind, he can deal spiritually with the heartbreaks and aches of this world, knowing this living hope of an inheritance is ready to be revealed in the last time.

God's power will keep the inheritance. God's power will call you, save you, keep you until the end of your salvation which will come when you leave this corruptible body to receive the inheritance *"reserved in heaven."*

A persecuted person cast adrift as a refugee in a foreign land may fear to place his hope in anything. It hurts when hopes are dashed and one may not want to hurt again, therefore we have this reminder of the power of God which will keep us until the end.

Peter piles word upon word, assurance upon assurance, to establish the utter reliability of the believer's basic hope. This hope can only be rejected by rejecting the Gospel itself and verse five lets us know a true believer will never do that.

WE CAN GREATLY REJOICE IN SUFFERING

"Wherein ye greatly rejoice, though now for a season, if need be, ye are in heaviness through manifold temptations".
—I Peter 1:6

The assurance that true believers have, causes them to rejoice, even in the midst of suffering. As heirs they can rejoice because their inheritance is protected and they are kept by the power of God for their present condition. They were to rejoice even in their present situation: *"in heaviness through manifold temptations".*

The excellence and assurance of their spiritual state did not exempt them, and does not exempt us from suffering in this world. When we are *"in heaviness through manifold temptations"* our spirits can be affected and sadness could overtake us, and sin can affect us unless someone reminds us of the short duration of suffering and the eternal provisions of God. For God knows when our spirits are ready to fail, not from weakness, but from strength. I Corinthians 10:13: *"There hath no temptation taken you but such as is common to man: but God is faithful, who will not suffer you*

45

to be tempted above that ye are able to bear it". Romans 8:18: *"For I reckon that the sufferings of this present time are not worthy to be compared with the glory which shall be revealed in us."*

OUR TRIALS OF FAITH WILL BE MADE PRAISE, HONOR, AND GLORY AT THE APPEARING OF JESUS CHRIST

"That the trial of your faith, Being much more precious than of gold that perisheth, though it be tried with fire, might be found unto praise and honor and glory at the appearing of Jesus Christ."

—I Peter 1:7

Therefore, we should greatly rejoice, even though sad, because of suffering, that we might realize (verse 7) the results of the trials of our faith—that precious faith that is more valuable than gold. This is gold that has been melted down to remove all impurities, and so the relationship between trials and faith. When faith is tried, impurities are removed, or it is found to be no faith. If a reminder of the rich and sure inheritance does not bring at least a little joy, our faith is no faith. But true faith is found unto praise, and prevents those that have it from fainting under pressure.

Psalm 27:13: *"I had fainted, unless I had believed to see the goodness of the Lord in the land of the living."* This is true that faith, even in the most difficult situations, will cause you to *"Wait on the Lord: be of good courage, and he shall strengthen thine heart: wait I say, on the Lord"* (Psalm 27:14).

TRUE FAITH COMES FROM HEARING THE WORD OF GOD

Romans 10:17: *"So then faith cometh by hearing and hearing by the word of God."* For this reason, faith is a jewel that can never be lost. It is a gift of God and the gifts of God are without repentance (Romans 11:29). So glorious shall be the reward that Christ shall bestow upon those who have been faithful to him under trial that words cannot describe it.

THE EFFECTS OF FAITH

"Whom having not seen, ye love; in whom, though now ye see him not, yet believing, ye rejoice with joy unspeakable and full of glory; receiving the end of your faith, even the salvation of your souls."

—I Peter 1:8 & 9

Let's look in verses eight and nine at the happy effects of faith on the believers that had been tried:

First, *it made them love Jesus Christ even though they had not seen Him.* Peter saw Him and believed, but Jesus Christ said to Thomas in John 20:29, *"...blessed are they that have not seen, and yet have believed."* The faith of Peter's readers caused them to love the Lord Jesus Christ even though they had not seen him.

Second, in the exercising of their faith, even though Jesus' bodily presence was not with them, *they followed Him and rejoiced with joy that was first unspeakable.* There were no words to express the nature, height, or depth of this joy. It was also the beginning of that joy which glorified spirits have in Heaven. When one glorifies God in the midst of trials, I believe that they will break forth with such expressions of joy that even they will be surprised.

When my dear wife was suffering through the difficulties that are

47

associated with being treated for cancer, she would listen to Christian tapes that would make her laugh. When she was too sick to laugh, it was my turn to laugh for her and to remind her that she would laugh again. When you trust in the Lord in the midst of trials you will be surprised at the expressions of joy He will place in your heart. Joy that must be expressed as the old hymn says: *"I said I wasn't going to tell nobody, but I just could not keep it to myself; what the Lord has done for me."*

The third effect of faith *is the right to, and a taste of eternal salvation which is here called* **"the end of your faith."** When we receive Christ on His terms, we have His assurance that God hath **"raised us up together, and make us sit together in heavenly places in Christ Jesus."**

The saved have everlasting life and occasionally taste what heaven is like. When I was a child the people in my community had a hard life, but it did not hinder them from expressing their joy for the provisions of God, nor did it hinder shouts of praise in the midst of the congregation—it was a taste of heaven. That faith, which by trials is discovered to be sound, is the faith by which believers receive the salvation of their souls.

These nine verses of I Peter are just a taste of what Peter has in store for the careful reader. His readers were real people just like us, who made a decision to trust the Lord Jesus for eternity. It may be that you are having a tough time right now. Bring things into focus through I Peter 1:13; clear your mind of trash so the holiness of God can cheer your heart.

BRINGING OTHERS TO JESUS

Pastor Carl Bennett

Pastor Carl Bennett has served as an associate pastor at
Eagleview Baptist Church, Adventure Baptist Church, and
Faithworks Community Church.

*"And again he [Jesus] entered into Capernaum after some
days; and it was noised that he was in the house. And
straightway many were gathered together, insomuch that there
was no room to receive them, no, not so much as about the
door: and he preached the word unto them. And they come
unto him, bringing one sick of the palsy, which was borne of
four. And when they could not come nigh unto him for the
press, they uncovered the roof where he was: and when they
had broken it up, they let down the bed wherein the sick of
the palsy lay. When Jesus saw their faith, he said unto the
sick of the palsy, Son, thy sins be forgiven thee. But there
were certain of the scribes sitting there, and reasoning in
their hearts, Why doth this man thus speak blasphemies?
who can forgive sins but God only? And immediately when
Jesus perceived in his spirit that they so reasoned within
themselves, he said unto them, Why reason ye these things
in your hearts? Whether is it easier to say to the sick of the
palsy, Thy sins be forgiven thee; or to say, Arise, and take up
thy bed, and walk? But that ye may know that the Son of
man hath power on earth to forgive sins, (he saith to the sick
of the palsy,) I say unto thee, Arise, and take up thy bed, and
go thy way into thine house. And immediately he arose, took
up the bed, and went forth before them all; insomuch that
they were all amazed, and glorified God, saying, We never
saw it on this fashion."* —Mark 2:1-12

Jesus Christ is the only true Saviour. He is the only One Who can forgive sin so that one can spend eternity in heaven.

This message is about soul-winning. Hopefully, it will encourage the saints to bring others to Jesus. Soul-winning fulfills the Great Commission: *"And Jesus came and spake unto them, saying, All power is given unto me in heaven and in earth. Go ye therefore, and teach all nations, baptizing them in the name of the Father, and of the Son, and of the Holy Ghost; Teaching them to observe all things whatsoever I have commanded you; and, lo, I am with you alway, even unto the end of the world. Amen"* (Matthew 28:18-20).

Soul-winning is a function of the church: *"Praising God, and having favour with all the people. And the Lord added to the church daily such as should be saved"* (Acts 2:47). And soul-winning puts saints in line for the soul-winners' crown *"For what is our hope, or joy, or crown of rejoicing? Are not even ye in the presence of our Lord Jesus at his coming? For ye are his glory and joy"* (I Thessalonians 2:19-20).

Notice these verses from the Word of God about soul-winning:

"He that winneth souls is wise."
—Proverbs 11:30

"Let him know, that he which converteth the sinner from the error of his way shall save a soul from death, and shall hide a multitude of sin."
—James 5:20

"Likewise, I say unto you, there is joy in the presence of the angels of God over one sinner that repenteth."
—Luke 15:10

50

In the text, a paralyzed man was brought to Jesus. This paralytic was spiritually healed, *"Son, thy sins be forgiven thee"* (vs. 5); and physically healed, *"I say unto thee, Arise, and take up thy bed, and go thy way into thine house. And immediately he arose, took up the bed, and went forth before them all"* (vs. 11-12).

There were many who brought others to Jesus such as the "centurion" (Matthew 8:5), "a woman of Canaan" (Matthew 15:22), and "great multitudes" (Matthew 15:30-31). The saints should bring others to Jesus as they have a need that can only be met by Jesus. The challenge of today is to bring others to Jesus—tell somebody about the saving grace of Jesus.

IT WAS NOISED THAT HE WAS IN THE HOUSE

The people reported that Jesus was in the house. It is always good when the saints are talking about Jesus. Talking about the true and living Savior is the business of the saints. The saints should be talking about Jesus anywhere and everywhere with anybody and everybody. The saints should witness about Jesus to their neighbors, friends, co-workers, creditors, family members, and other individuals. The saints should tell the good news that Jesus Christ is alive, liveth forever and wants to be the Saviour of every man.

THE RESULT OF THE WITNESS OF
THESE PEOPLE WAS...

Many responded immediately to the report that Jesus was in the house to the point that the house was filled. The house was filled to the point that there was no room to receive them, *"no, not so much as about the door."*

51

The crowd went to the house to see Jesus. Those who made the report about Jesus being in the house, actually followed God's plan for soul-winning—*"Go out into all the highways and hedges and compel them to come in, that my house may be filled"*(Luke 14:23).

HE PREACHED THE WORD UNTO THEM

Jesus did not preach to entertain. He preached the gospel unto those in the house. The gospel is that God's only Son provides eternal life.

Saints should always preach and teach the Word of God. They should not sugarcoat the Gospel or say what someone wants to hear. Saints should tell the unsaved about the new birth (John 3:1-16), Heaven and Hell (Luke 16:19-31), salvation (Romans 10:8-13), and the Second Coming of Christ (Titus 2:13). Saints should teach and preach *"That Christ died for our sins according to the scriptures; And that He was buried, and that He rose again the third day according to the Scriptures"* (I Corinthians 15:3-4).

"For I am not ashamed of the Gospel of Christ: for it is the power of God unto salvation to every one that believeth; to the Jew first, and also to the Greek" (Romans1:16).

Preach the word — Preach the word — Preach the word!

BORNE OF FOUR SOUL-WINNERS

"And they come unto Him, bringing one sick of the palsy, which was borne of four" (Mark 2:3).

52

This man who was *"sick of the palsy"* was also spiritually paralyzed. He was helpless as he did not know the way to Jesus. Saints should pray for those who are unsaved and in need of the Savior, Jesus Christ, such as their relatives and friends, those on drugs and alcohol, those who are infected with AIDS, as well as members of cults.

Philip *"preached unto him* [the Ethiopian] *Jesus...and he answered and said, I believe that Jesus Christ is the Son of God"* (Acts 8:35-37). Philip brought the Ethiopian to the Lord Jesus Christ as he did not understand what he was reading from the *"prophet Esaias."* The Ethiopian *"desired Philip that he would come up and sit with him"* (Acts 8:26-31). Philip took advantage of the opportunity to bring the Ethiopian to Jesus Christ. Bringing others to Christ is the duty of all saints.

The four soul-winners in the text showed care, love, concern and compassion for their friend by bringing him to Jesus for healing. They realized that their friend was helpless and couldn't come to Jesus on his own.

Soul-winners for Christ should not be intimidated because of a person's status or position in life. Soul-winners should witness to all people—bank presidents, college professors, high school principals, pilots, military personnel, custodians, store clerks, and individuals at the bus stops.

Soul-winners should not be ashamed to witness because they will be talked about or made fun of because of their past or any other circumstances. After the woman had an encounter with Christ at the well, she went into the city and told the men, *"Come, see a Man, which told me all things that ever I did: is not this the Christ? Then they went out of the city and came unto him. Many of the Samaritans of that city believed on him for the saying of the woman, which testified, He told me all that ever I did"* (John 4:1-42). This woman was not ashamed to share the gospel message of Christ as prior to her encounter with Christ she was known to be living in sin.

Saints are to love all people and to have a burden for lost people. Saints are to show sinners that they are unsaved and on their way to hell. However, there is a way out of hell through the blood of Jesus. Saints should use the Bible to show a person to the Lord.

THE ROMAN ROAD

The saints should show the lost person the following:

1. *"As it is written, there is none righteous, no, not one"* (Romans 3:10).

2. *"For all have sinned and come short of the glory of God"* (Romans 3:23).

3. *"But God commendeth His love toward us, in that, while we were yet sinners, Christ died for us"* (Romans 5:8).

4. *"That if thou shalt confess with thy mouth the Lord Jesus, and shalt believe in thine heart that God hath raised him from the dead, thou shalt be saved"* (Romans 10:9).

5. *"For whosoever shall call upon the name of the Lord shall be saved"* (Romans 10:3).

PRAYER TO ACCEPT JESUS AS SAVIOUR

Dear God, I know I have sinned and I want to ask for your forgiveness. I believe that Jesus died for my sins. I now accept Your offer of eternal salvation. I will follow Jesus as my Saviour and try to obey Him in all that I do. Thank you for my new life. In the name of Jesus, I pray. Amen.

The four soul-winners in the text, worked together as a team to get the paralytic won to Jesus. They were committed to getting this man to Jesus.

The paralytic was carried by the four who came to the house which was filled, *"insomuch that there was no room to receive them, no, not so much as about the door"* (v.2). They could have very easily went back home with the man because of the crowd. However, because of their commitment, they got this man to Jesus by uncovering the roof and letting him down into the house. When Jesus saw their faith and commitment, *"he said unto the sick of the palsy, Son thy sins be forgiven thee"* (v.5).

Saints should continue knocking on doors even when they are rejected or persecuted. Saints should continue praying for the lost—never give up on anyone—continue praying that they will come to Jesus. If one method of evangelism does not work, try another Biblical method. Keep trying to get the unsaved to Jesus.

WHEN PEOPLE ACCEPT CHRIST, THE RELIGIOUS WILL QUESTION THE RESULTS

In the text, there are those trying to hinder God's work such as the crowd in the house and around the door. This crowd was not concerned about those who really needed to hear the Word of God.

The woman with the issue of blood for twelve years had to fight her way through the crowd to get to Jesus so that she could be healed. This woman heard about Jesus and did not allow the crowd to stop her (Mark 5:25-34).

Blind Bartimaeus heard that Jesus was passing by and cried out, *"Jesus, thou son of David, have mercy on me."* The crowd told him to *"hold his peace: but he cried the more a great deal, thou son of David, have mercy on me"* (Mark 10:46-52). Some saints are like the crowds in the situations of the woman with the issue of blood and blind Bartimaeus. They are not concerned about kingdom growth and are hindering or attempting to hinder others from coming to Jesus.

Jesus was criticized and accused of blasphemies as the scribes thought that only God could forgive sin. They did not know that Jesus is God.

Some saints will criticize the saved such as "that so and so town drunk is now preaching." The saved should pattern after the paralytic after his salvation: He *"went before them all; insomuch that they were amazed and glorified God saying, we never saw it on this fashion"* (v.12).

Soul-winners are needed today to deliver the message that Jesus died for sins and is the only way to eternal life (John 14:6). Saints should tell others that the Lord saved them and what He is doing in there lives.

CONCLUSION

The saints should bring others to Christ because there is a call:

1. There is a call from the _outside_, based on the fact that those without Christ are lost.

2. There is a call from the _inside_, based on the debt we owe because we have heard the gospel and everyone deserves to hear it.

3. There is a call from _above_, because Christ is the only way of salvation.

4. There is a call from the _future_, based on the shortness of time to decide.

In closing, let me share something with you. The following was penned by a young pastor in Africa:

MY COMMITMENT AS A CHRISTIAN

I'm part of the fellowship of the unashamed. I have stepped over the line. The decision has been made. I'm a disciple of Jesus Christ. I won't look back, let up, slow down, back away, or be still. My past is redeemed, my present makes sense, my future is secure. I'm finished and done with low living, sight walking, small planning, smooth knees, colorless dreams, tamed visions, mundane talking, cheap living, and dwarfed goals.

I no longer need preeminence, prosperity, position, promotions, plaudits, or popularity. I don't have to be right, first, tops, recognized, praised, regarded, or rewarded. I now live by faith, lean on His presence, walk by patience, lift by prayer, and labor by power.

My face is set, my gait is fast, my goal is Heaven, my road is narrow, my way rough, my companions few, my Guide reliable, *my mission clear. I cannot be bought, deluded, or delayed. I will not flinch in the face of sacrifice, hesitate in the presence of the adversary, negotiate at the table of the enemy, or meander in the maze of mediocrity.*

I won't give up, shut up, let up, until I have stayed up, stored up, prayed up, paid up, and preached up for the cause of Christ. I am a disciple of Jesus. I must go till He comes, give till I drop, preach till all know, and work till He stops me. And when He comes for His own, He will have no problem recognizing me — my banner will be clear!

THE IMPORTANCE OF REACHING THE INNER-CITIES

Pastor Victor Rivera

Pastor Victor Rivera is the pastor of the Christ Independent Baptist Church in Philadelphia, Pennsylvania.

"Go ye into all the world, and preach the gospel to every creature."
—Mark 16:15

The Bible commands the Christian to *"Go ye into ALL the world..."* (Mark 16:15). This includes the places where the rich, the well-to-do, as well as the impoverished live. That includes the inner-cities.

I am amazed to hear that church planting should take place where those reached have a financial ability to support the new church, thus enabling the church to become self-supporting quicker and then in turn, reach into the inner-city nearest the church. This may sound logical to the modern mind but this is not Bible. The Bible says, *"Go ye into ALL the world..."* (Mark 16:15).

As we look at church planting in the Bible we find the missionary, Apostle Paul, going into the inner-cities of his day and starting new churches. Acts 18:1-11 is one of several occasions where we find Paul starting a new church within an inner-city.

Why then, is it important to reach the inner-cities? Simply stated, the Bible commands the Christian to *"Go ye into ALL the world..."* (Mark 16:15). This is a matter of obedience, not convenience. Will

59

we be obedient to the Word of God or not? Has God changed the marching orders for the Christians? No, I don't think so. So then, has God given up on the inner-cities as some of our brethren have? No, again. God is still calling men and anointing them to *"Go ye..."* (Mark 16:15). God is still telling them the same thing He told the missionary Apostle Paul:

"Be not afraid, but speak...for I am with thee, and no man shall set on thee to hurt thee: for I have much people in this city."
—Acts 18:9-10

This being true, why is there such difficulty finding men who are convinced of God's calling to the inner-cities? The answer is the same carnal problem experienced by Christians of the first century in Jerusalem. They had been commanded to *"...wait for the promise of the Father...the Holy Ghost..."* (Acts 1:4-5), and then **GO**. They received the promise (Acts 2), but then continued staying in Jerusalem until God had to send *"a great persecution against the church which was at Jerusalem; and they were all scattered abroad throughout the regions of Judea and Samaria"* (Acts 8:1).

The Christians in Jerusalem had received God's marching orders to *"Go ye into ALL the world..."* (Mark 16:15) but instead, they remained in their comfortable, safe, familiar haven. So God had to send persecution which helped to convince His people to **GO**.

In the same manner, we find great spiritual centers throughout America's suburbs while many of her inner-cities are spiritual deserts, which desperately need the Living Water.

60

Where are the men of God? They are continuing to study at these great spiritual centers, receiving more and more instruction, while becoming more and more deaf to the call of God to the inner-cities.

If we are ever going to see a revival in our great land, we must begin to see that we have neglected a vast mission field within our own borders. Could it be that revival tarries, not only because of the prayerless church, but also because of the prejudiced church that has neglected most of our inner-cities?

The word "prejudiced" is used to denote the attitude of many toward the diverse and different people who dwell in the inner-cities. Because they are different, it is easier, and some think safer, to stay out of and away from these places. The importance of reaching these inner-cities is not only to be obedient to the Word of God, but also to be obedient to the work of the Spirit of God which lusts against the flesh.

"For the flesh lusteth against the Spirit, and the Spirit against the flesh: and these are contrary the one to the other: so that ye cannot do the things that ye would."
—Galatians 5:17

The prejudiced heart is a partial heart (James 2:4), a condition that affects all of us. But we must remember that when a person gets saved he becomes a new creature in Christ, all things become new—"ALL things" include how we view people who are different.

There are many battles that a new Christian must fight, and one of these is the battle "to whom will I yield?" To the Holy Ghost or to sinful flesh? The Bible says that there is *"...no respect of persons with God"* (Romans 2:11). This being the case, partiality is a fruit of the flesh, not the Spirit. The matter of reaching the inner-cities has been hindered by the Christians and churches who have yielded to the flesh rather than the Spirit of God. Many of these churches have great missions programs, but at the same time neglect lost people right around their church building or in nearby inner-cities. Why? Simply because those living in the inner-cities are DIFFERENT?

If *"God is not willing that any should perish, but that all should come to repentance"* (II Peter 3:9), and if His command is still *"Go ye into ALL the world, and preach the gospel to EVERY creature"* (Mark 16:15), then the inner-cities of America must be of utmost importance to God. Men of God must be willing to get into (not avoid) these financially strapped areas and live among (not separate from) the people who may be different. This is God's will and this is God's call!

HOW TO KEEP
YOUR DREAMS ALIVE

Dr. Kevin D. Barnes, Sr.

Dr. Kevin D. Barnes, Sr. is the pastor of the Abyssinian Missionary Baptist Church in Oakland, California.

My brothers and sisters, each of us have something in common, and that is, all of us have dreams. It does not matter who you are, each of us have dreams. Some of our dreams are shattered dreams, some are fulfilled dreams, and some are small dreams; still others are large dreams. In fact, some are past dreams, and yes, some are present dreams. We all have some dreams. Even children have dreams, and many of them dream of who they can become. Actually, we kind of help them with their dreams. The other day, one of the kids said to me, "Pastor, do you know what I want to be when I grow up?" I said, "No." He said, "I want to be a pastor." He had a dream.

Not only do our children have dreams, but I have discovered that even our communities have dreams. It does not matter where you live, on the south side, the north side, or the west side, our dream is to have a better community. We are tired of the black on black crime that is plaguing our communities, so, we too, dream of safer communities. Then not only do the children have dreams, and our communities have dreams, but even the churches have dreams, and our dream is to save the lost at any cost.

Now watch this, there are two kinds of dreams: one refers to those powerful images we have when we are asleep—that something we do not remember, and the other kind of dream is about our aspirations, goals, and future visions. I want to talk to you about

"How to Keep Your Dreams Alive." There are things you must know: (1) Know you have to be different. (2) Know that you will be treated differently, and (3) Know that you will rise differently. Look at the text in Genesis 37, verses 1 through 5. The text begins with, *"And Jacob..."* *And* is a conjunction, so, therefore, before we can deal with Chapter 37, there has to be other things that come before it.

Well verse 1 says, *"And Jacob dwelt in the land wherein his father was a stranger, in the land of Canaan."* It tells us where Jacob lived, but, verse two is the key: *"These are the generations of Jacob. Joseph, being seventeen years old...."* So the text is really about Joseph, but now this was not the first time that we hear of Joseph, for in Chapter 30, verses 22-24, Jacob's favorite wife, Rachel, has his favorite son, Joseph. Rachel had been barren for many years, and even though Jacob had four wives (Leah, Bilhah, Zilpah, and Rachel), Rachel was his favorite wife.

The second mention of Joseph is in Genesis 33:2. Jacob's brother, Esau and four hundred men were approaching the camp of Jacob; so, to protect the camp, Jacob placed Rachel and Joseph at the rear of the camp so that if anything happened, they could get to safety quickly.

Then the third time we see Joseph is in Genesis 33:7. Rachel and Joseph are brought to meet with Uncle Esau and they bow down to Esau. Joseph had been taught some manners, which in our society is rare. However, Joseph was different. We see Joseph again in Chapter 36, verse 24 when Joseph is simply listed in the registry of Jacob's sons.

Then, finally, we come to Chapter 37 in verse 2, where Joseph is seventeen years old, out feeding the flock of his father with some of his stepbrothers. The text says that Joseph brought his father an evil report concerning his brothers. Now there are some that would accuse Joseph of being a tattletale, but that was not the case for three reasons: (1) Tattle tales do not tell the truth, they always like to add to the truth. (2) It was Joseph's job to tell, and (3) Joseph was obligated to his father. As Christians, we are also obligated to our Heavenly Father. Now watch this, out of all of Jacob's sons the text says "Jacob loved Joseph more than all his children because he was the son of his old age."

Now if Jacob loved Joseph more than all of his other children, that would be a problem because Jacob had another son after Joseph, named Benjamin. Well Joseph, the son of his old age, in Hebrew, means a "wise son;" one who possesses wisdom above his years. **First, Joseph was different**. He was wise at a young age and that tells us you do not have to be old to be wise. Joseph was a type of Christ. Jesus was only 33 years old and look what he accomplished.

> When man was hungry, who fed them?
> When man was thirsty, who gave them water?
> When man was lost, Jesus became the bright and morning star.
> When man was sick, Jesus became the great physician.
> When man was lonely, Jesus became a friend that sticks closer than a brother.
> When man was burdened down, Jesus became a burden bearer.
> When man was in darkness, Jesus became the light of the world.

The text says Jacob gave Joseph a coat of many colors. The coat symbolized leadership. Joseph was a leader. My brothers and sisters, if you are going to keep your dreams alive, you must be different.

My brother Herbert is 65 years old and he had to ask me, his baby brother, for spiritual counseling. He knew that spiritually, his baby brother, was wiser than he was.

Then second, **Joseph was treated differently** (see verse 4). The text says his brothers saw how daddy loved him more. They hated him. Do you know that people will treat you different because you are blessed? Sometimes friends, you know those that smile in your face and all the time are trying to take your place—backstabbers. Can I tell you not everybody is excited about your success, and because people are not excited, they will treat you differently.

Watch this, I can understand sometimes why my friends do not like me, because I do not have many friends. I just have associates, but that is okay. They never liked me so that does not matter, but when it comes to family, for you see the text says, Joseph's *brothers* hated him. They hated their own brother. They were full of animosity, they detested him, disliked him intensely, they were sickened by Joseph. His own brothers hated him. No doubt when the other brothers got together on Memorial Day to barbeque, they would not invite Joseph. When, or if their wives would have his nephew, they would not even tell him the child's name. When the brother's family got together on Christmas, and everybody put their name in the hat to pull names; they would not have his name in the hat. When their kids graduated from high school, Joseph would not get an invitation. They hated him.

However, notice in verse six, Joseph says, *"I pray you,"* in other words, you might not want to hear my prayers, but I will tell you anyway. I told you that Joseph was a type of Christ, who died and was buried, but rose from the dead. In addition, if you are going to keep your dreams alive, you have to know Jesus.

> Abraham knew Him as the sacrifice.
> Moses knew Him as the pillar of cloud.
> Aaron knew Him as the rod that budded.
> Gideon knew Him as the angel of the Lord.

Ruth knew Him as the kingdom redeemer.
Samuel knew Him as the Ark of the Covenant.
Elijah knew Him as the still small voice.
Ezekiel knew Him as a wheel in the middle of a wheel
Isaiah knew Him as the high and lifted up.
Nevertheless, I know Him as my all and all.

There was an old woman with children who she was sick. The oldest boy went to the mother and said, "Momma, we don't have any food in the cupboard, what are we going to do." The old lady said, "Son help me to the window." The old woman sat at the window, looked out, and said three words, "Lord, you promised." She then walked back to her bed. After a while, the son went back to the window and said, "Momma, we still don't have any food and all you said was, "Lord you promised." After this, there was a loud crash in front of the house. There was a truck outside. The wind trailer of the truck fell over, and there was ham, potatoes, beans, and rice right in front of the house. The driver of the truck said, "You can have all you can pick up." The kids adopted character because they remembered what momma said, "Lord, you promised." Whatever your dreams are, hold on, help is on the way.

If God said it, that settles it.

Keep your dreams alive.

WHEN THE LORD'S BRIDE AND THE PASTOR'S BRIDE DON'T COINCIDE

Dr. Lynwood Davis

Dr. Lynwood Davis is the pastor of the Northeast Baptist Temple in Baltimore, Maryland.

In Judges Chapter 14, young Samson married a young girl of the Philistines. At the wedding feast, Samson and the young men started boasting and bragging about their ability. Samson put their wisdom to the test by giving them a riddle. He also gave them seven days to solve it. The young men labored for three days to solve the riddle, but to no avail. They felt compelled to solve Samson's riddle. They could not let this muscle-bound Jewish boy come into their neighborhood, and make them look foolish. They had to solve this riddle at any cost.

In verse 15, the young men used the same approach Satan used to cause Adam to stumble.

"And it came to past on the seventh day, that they said unto Samson's wife, Entice thy husband, that he may declare unto us his riddle, lest we burn thee and thy father's house with fire: have ye called us to take that we have? is it not so? And Samson's wife wept before him, and said, Thou dost hate me, and lovest me not: thou hast put forth a riddle unto the children of my people, and hast not told it me. And he said unto her, Behold I have not told it my father nor my mother, and shall I tell it thee? And she wept before him seven days, while their feast lasted: and it came to pass on the seventh day, that he told her, because she lay sore upon him: and she

told the riddle to the children of her people."

—Judges 14:15-17

The young men knew that they could not equal Samson's wisdom and might. So, they turned to Samson's wife. They said, "Mrs. Samson, if you don't give us the answer to the riddle, we're going to burn your father's house."

Mrs. Samson questioned Samson until he told her the answer to the riddle. She immediately told the young men the answer. Please don't blame her for what she did to Samson. The blame lies with Samson.

Samson did not setup good communication in his relationship with his wife. He did not protect her, nor did he assure her of his uncompromising support. There was no trust in their relationship. Samson's lack of giving quality time to his wife forced her to take matters into her own hands.

On the seventh day, the young men told Samson the answer to the riddle, Samson, realizing what they did, had this to say, *"If ye had not plowed with my heifer, ye had not found out my riddle"* (Judges 14:18b).

According to *Genesis' Hebrew-Chaldee Lexicon to the Old Testament*, "plow" means to cut into. Samson is implying that the young men devised and made things to "cut into" his wife. Such "cutting" was more than she could bear. Thus she reacted against her husband.

Pastors and full-time Christian workers, you need to understand what Samson is saying. It is a message that applies to our ministry and families. You need to listen carefully. Samson is saying, "If you had not been so disrespectful to my wife, if you had not discouraged her, you would have never found my weakness. You found my weakness by 'cutting into' my wife with things she could not deal with."

There is a growing number of pastors' wives who are leaving, or thinking about leaving their husbands. They, like Mrs. Samson, can't deal with the constant "plowing" they are facing. So, they leave their husbands. They are not reacting to what their husbands are doing, but to his lack of protection against her plowers.

What is the problem? Why are so many pastors' wives hurting? I believe someone is doing to pastors' wives what Samson said the young men did to his wife—plowing with the heifer. They were rude and disrespectful to her. She became a discouraged and miserable woman. She wept and cried before Samson for seven days. Finally, he told her the answer to the riddle.

Samson found out too late that the young men had plowed with his wife. By the time it was revealed to him, she had already surrendered to the pressure of her plowers. It was the plowing of the young men who destroyed Rev. and Mrs. Samson's relationship.

Preachers, please listen to what I'm saying. Satan has not changed. He plows with our wives to create a spiritual ineffectiveness in our ministries. Adam lost his spiritual effectiveness by not protecting Eve from the plowing of Satan. Failure to protect your wife from the plowers will destroy your spiritual effectiveness. Don't say it can't happen to you, because it's happening in Bible-believing churches all across America. Pastors' wives are leaving their husbands.

HOW DOES SATAN PLOW WITH
THE PASTOR'S WIFE?

Preachers are responsible for two women: his bride, and the Lord's bride. And sometimes, Satan skillfully gets the Lord's bride to go against the preacher's bride so they don't coincide. The person Satan uses to plow with the pastors' wife is oftentimes the church which the pastor oversees. Often, the pastor's wife is like the comedian, Rodney Dangerfield, who says, "I get no respect."

MANY CHURCHES MISTREAT AND DISHONOR
THE PASTOR'S WIFE

Margaret and I travel to different churches to strengthen and encourage families. We were so surprised at some of the things the Lord's bride is putting the Pastor's bride through. One pastor's wife was physically attacked by a lady in the church. Church members observe and talk about the preacher's wife more than any other woman in the church. Something is always wrong with her. If she gets upset, she is hotheaded. If she wears her dress too long, she is old fashion and out of touch. If her dress is short, she is not a good example for the church. If she fails to speak to everyone, she is stuck up. If she misses church, she is worldly. Something is always wrong with the preacher's wife.

Church members plow at the preacher's wife by making cruel statements to her, and about her. One pastor bought his wife a car. One of the ladies of the church made the statement, in the presence of his wife, "I'm tired of always paying for the pastor's wife's car." The pastor's wife dropped her head and walked away dejected.

Many women in the church compete with the preacher's wife for her husband's attention. Women call her house all hours of the night with trivial problems. In church, they are always honoring and congratulating him for something, and walk by her as if she does not exist.

PASTORS NEED TO FACE THEIR WIVES' GRIEVANCES

When the church plows with the pastor's wife, she turns to her husband for comfort and protection. He dishonors her by not taking the time to comfort and encourage her. It is crushing to a pastor's wife to turn to her husband for help, but he is too busy helping others. This is one of the reasons so many pastors' wives are leaving home.

She, like all wives, wants security from her husband. She wants assurance that he is committed to love and support her with whatever difficulty she faces. She isn't asking him to abandon his church for her. She just wants assurance that, when the Lord's bride mistreats her, he will work with her to solve the problem.

Security means that they, the pastor and his wife, are committed to supporting and protecting each other, no matter what. This means that we must listen to our wives' grievances without lecturing them. We must give our wives quality time to share their feelings, hopes, dreams and fears with us.

Several problems will develop when a pastor fails to give his wife the security she needs:

First, **issues are constantly raised, but never resolved**. You talk about issues that are important to her, but you can never resolve anything. Frustrations build up and you stop talking to each other. This forces you to put on a front in the presence of your people. In church you are the perfect couple, while at home there is a power struggle going on.

Second, **you will abandon the idea of solving issues, and start blaming each other**. You make unkind and insensitive statements to each other. You try to provoke, or force the other person to change.

Third, **you stop attacking each other, and attack the marriage relationship**. You start thinking to yourself, "What am I doing in this marriage?" "How can I get out of this no win relationship?" Once you question your relationship, your marriage is in serious trouble. The wife slowly leaves her husband and the ministry. Preacher, you need to listen to your wife's grievances.

Please don't limit this problem to the black preacher. The white preacher is experiencing the same problem, only in a different way. When the church plows with his wife, he convinces her to endure the plowing. He's afraid it will hurt or destroy the ministry. So, she holds her hurt in because she doesn't want to hurt her husband's ministry. He spends many hours building up the homes of his church, but has no time to address his wife's grievances. So, she holds her hurt on the inside.

It is not so with the wives of black preachers. Many black sisters will not hold their hurt on the inside for the sake of the ministry; many will pack their bags and leave!

Pastors need to take time away from the Lord's bride to build

up and encourage his bride. The only vacation many of our wives
ever have is when we take them to a preacher's fellowship meeting.
Isn't that romantic?

PASTORS NEED TO HONOR THEIR
WIVES PUBLICLY

*"Likewise, ye husbands, dwell with them according to
knowledge, giving honour unto the wife, as unto the weaker
vessel, and as being heirs together of the grace of life; that
your prayers be not hindered."*

—I Peter 3:7

One of the most devastating things that can occur in marriage
is for the husband to become critical of his wife. He cannot
afford to treat her with scorn, or be sarcastic toward her. A
wise pastor will make his wife feel important to him and to his ministry.
Often, the pastor's wife feels that the church is the only important
thing in his life. Thus, she is threatened at the very core of life.

The Bible says that the husband is to place value upon his wife
by honoring her. I believe this honoring goes beyond the
confines of the home, and into the church. The wise pastor will
honor his wife from the pulpit. He knows that it will teach his
people to honor and respect her also. The church will honor
whom the pastor honors. When he makes good statements about
her from the pulpit, it teaches the people to say good statements
about her also. When a church dishonors and plows with the
preacher's wife, it's usually because he gives her no honor in
their presence. The church honors whom the pastor honors.

Pastors need to build up their brides from the pulpit. If we don't
honor our wives, we can't expect the church to honor them.

When you fail to honor your wife, you make her feel inferior, and doubtful. She develops a demanding nature. She will go out of her way to avoid personal involvement with you and the church. Next thing you know, she is packing her bags. Pastors, you must teach the Lord's bride to honor your time with your bride. You need to spend quality time with her. Listen to what she has to say. Protect her from the plowers. She is worth it.

No one plows with Margaret Davis without plowing with me. She is my mirror. When I look at her, she always has a warm and loving expression about her, and that encourages my soul. It makes me feel brand new. I could never allow anyone to plow with, or dishonor Margaret.

If you are wondering whether or not Samson ever changed his ways with Mrs. Samson, the answer is NO! She ran off with his best friend. *"But Samson's wife was given to his companion, whom he had used as his friend"* (Judges 14:20).

If you are a pastor's wife, I know how frustrating it must be. However, you need to understand the tremendous pressure your husband is under. When he asks you what's wrong, please don't say, "Nothing." Tell him where it hurts. He will never understand what you are going through until you share it with him.

Pastors, set aside some time for you and your wife to get away. Taking her to the next fellowship meeting is not her idea of getting alone. She needs time to share herself with you. I'm fully aware of the demand on your time. However, what would it profit a pastor to solve all the problems of his church, and lose his wife in the process?

WAITING ON GOD

Pastor Tony Smart

Pastor Tony Smart is the pastor of the Victory Baptist Church in Tampa, Florida.

"To whom then will ye liken me, or shall I be equal? saith the Holy One. Lift up your eyes on high, and behold who hath created these things, that bringeth out their host by number: he calleth them all by names by the greatness of his might, for that he is strong in power; not one faileth. Why sayest thou, O Jacob, and speakest, O Israel, My way is hid from the LORD, and my judgement is passed over from my God? Hast thou not known? hast thou not heard, that the everlasting God, the LORD, the Creator of the ends of the earth, fainteth not, neither is weary? there is no searching of his understanding. He giveth power to the faint; and to them that have no might he increaseth strength. Even the youths shall faint and be weary, and the young men shall utterly fall: But they that wait upon the LORD shall renew their strength: they shall mount up with wings as eagles; they shall run, and not be weary; and they shall walk, and not faint."

—Isaiah 40:25-31

Today's message is entitled "Waiting on God." I believe it is one of the most significant aspects of Christian living that we must learn. It is imperative that believers understand that God's timing of events in our lives, the way He assigns priorities to our prayer requests, the time He chooses to lift certain burdens we bear, are all done with a good and higher purpose. I enjoy reading through a well written suspense novel and feeling the intensity of the plot building until one gets to the last chapter.

Throughout the reading one is given a sense of anticipation for what may happen next.

I believe so it is when we wait on God. His will for us unfolds over time and we never quite know all the details of His plan for us, but we can be assured that after we have prayed, and have been obedient to His revealed will, and doing those things which we know are right, God will direct us, and encourage us in ways unimaginable.

WAITING ON GOD IS:

1. **Expectation**: When the servant of God is truly relying on Him to accomplish great things there is daily expectation, even hour to hour expectation, that something unprecedented will occur. Servant of the Lord, you may rest assured that whatever your Heavenly Father sends your way will be of great value to you. The Bible tells us in James 1:17 that *"Every good gift and every perfect gift is from above, and cometh down from the Father of lights..."*

Yes, our adversary, the devil, will attempt to interfere with your faith and service when you make commitments to God. The more spiritually minded a servant of God becomes, the bigger a prize he becomes for the wicked one. Every satanic weapon ever devised may be directed at you—lies will be told about you, men will rise up against you—but through it all we should expect God to grant us the victory. People that wait on God are winners. The Psalmist tells us to *"Trust in the LORD, and do good; so shalt thou dwell in the land, and verily thou shalt be fed. Delight thyself also in the LORD; and he shall give thee the desires of thine heart. Commit thy way unto the LORD; trust also in him; and he shall bring it to pass"* (Psalm 37:3-5). Are you expecting God to do something unique and majestic in your midst?

2. **Exercising Patience**: Abraham's son, Ishmael, was born into this world partly because he and his wife, Sarah, became weary while waiting on God to give them the promised child, Isaac (Genesis 15:2-4, 16:1-16, 18:10-15, 21:12). Isaiah said that *"they that wait upon the Lord shall renew their strength..."*

While we are journeying through this life we may become tired at times, even right up to the point of calling it quits. I don't know of any bonafide servant of God who hasn't battled what I call acute fatigue. The ministry is a marathon, not a sprint, and God's timetable doesn't always agree with ours, but think of the blessings you have received which were directly related to your waiting on God to do something. Maybe it was the salvation of a loved one, a change in behavior of a teenaged child you have been praying for, the rekindled love of a spouse, a new open door opportunity to minister, or receipt of some material blessing. These are benefits obtained by patiently waiting on God, trusting Him for accomplishments beyond one's capability and what a joy it is when we see God's hand doing these things.

3. **Experience**: Before a person steps out by faith into a ministry, it is a real good idea for him to learn to wait on the Lord for proper instruction, direction, and provision. I can't over-emphasize that this is a learning process. Every servant of God will be trained by God through this waiting period. In Scripture we have the experiences of Joshua with Moses, Elisha with Elijah, the Apostles with the Lord Jesus, Timothy with Paul, and Ruth with Naomi.

After the servant of God gains the experience he needs by

waiting on God under a mentor, he is better prepared to serve the Lord in the field where he is called. If human employers require experience from job applicants, why shouldn't we believe that Almighty God wouldn't also demand His servants to gain experience? Young preachers learn extremely valuable lessons by learning to wait on God even before they start out in ministry. The initial experience may make the difference between a long and fruitful ministry and one that is short-lived.

4. **Examination**: While the servant of God is waiting on the LORD to provide encouragement to do the work, it is also a great time to do self-examination. We may ask, Is there anything in my life that would hinder God's Spirit from renewing my strength? Is my relationship right with my brothers and sisters in Christ? Do I harbor any unconfessed sin? Remember, John said in Revelation 2:21 (speaking of an individual in the Church at Thyatira) *"...I gave her space to repent of her fornication; and she repented not."*

Obviously, the time God allots us to prove His faithfulness also affords us the opportunity to get right and live right. Preacher, it is a crying shame when God can't trust someone with His refreshing power because of sin in that person's life, or because of a lack of integrity. Christians who are truly waiting for God to manifest His power in their lives, or through their ministries, take the opportunities they have to spread open their souls to the scrutiny of the Word of God and the Spirit of God, they also should welcome helpful criticism.

5. **Exaltation**: Now we get to the conclusion of the process of waiting on God. The scripture says: *"...they shall mount up with wings as eagles; they shall run and not be weary; and they shall walk, and not faint."* There is a sense of freedom and

grace gained exclusively by those, who in weakness and helplessness, turn to the God of the Bible. I am convinced that the works that are going to endure for all eternity are those ministries that are built by frail people who, perhaps at one time thought themselves stronger than they actually were, came to an end of self, then told God, "If YOU don't empower me to do it. I can't do it." They started out to do something great for God, then they learned that God really was doing something great through them. While they were waiting quietly, He equipped them to do more!

HELL! DO WE REALLY BELIEVE IT?

Daniel Whyte III

"There was a certain rich man, which was clothed in purple and fine linen, and fared sumptuously every day: And there was a certain beggar named Lazarus, which was laid at his gate, full of sores, And desiring to be fed with the crumbs which fell from the rich man's table: moreover the dogs came and licked his sores. And it came to pass, that the beggar died, and was carried by the angels into Abraham's bosom: the rich man also died, and was buried; And in hell he lift up his eyes, being in torments, and seeth Abraham afar off, and Lazarus in his bosom. And he cried and said, Father Abraham, have mercy on me, and send Lazarus, that he may dip the tip of his finger in water, and cool my tongue; for I am tormented in this flame. But Abraham said, Son, remember that thou in thy lifetime receivedst thy good things, and likewise Lazarus evil things: but now he is comforted, and thou art tormented. And beside all this, between us and you there is a great gulf fixed: so that they which would pass from hence to you cannot; neither can they pass to us, that would come from thence. Then he said, I pray thee therefore, father, that thou wouldest send him to my father's house: For I have five brethren; that he may testify unto them, lest they also come into this place of torment. Abraham saith unto him, They have Moses and the prophets; let them hear them. And he said, nay, father Abraham: but if one went unto them from the dead, they will repent. And he said unto him, if they hear not Moses and the prophets, neither will they be persuaded, though one rose from the dead."

—Luke 16:19-31

I am sure that you have heard the story about the atheist criminal who was on his way to be executed for a crime that he had committed. And following him, was a minister, who was reading from the Scriptures. And the criminal, who did not believe in God, turned around and said with fear on his face and a tremble in his voice, "Sir, if I believed in hell like you Christians say you do, I would crawl all over London, England on broken glass, warning every person of that place."

I believe that one of the major reasons why so many lost people don't get saved is because they really don't believe that there is a literal, burning hell. I am of the opinion that if one would really get a vision, a picture of this awful place called hell, they would get saved. I believe one of the reasons why so many of us Christians are not living the lives we ought to live is because we really don't believe that there is a hell. If we did, I think we would live differently for the sake of those who are lost. I also believe the reason why so many of us Christians are not engaged in the business of soul-winning as we ought to be, is because many of us really don't believe that there is a literal, burning hell. Oh, yes, we believe it theoretically, but I'm afraid that many of us don't believe it practically.

IS THERE REALLY A HELL?

First of all, I am moved to ask the question, *is there really a hell?* I know that this question may sound strange coming from a Baptist preacher to a Baptist crowd, but the question still remains— is there really a hell?

Well, if you believe that the Bible is the infallible Word of God, you have got to believe—you must believe—that there is a literal burning hell, where every person who dies without Christ will spend eternity, because the Bible is replete with the doctrine of hell. IS THERE A HELL? Listen to God's Word for an emphatic answer in the affirmative: Job said in Job 26:6, *"Hell is naked before him, and destruction hath no covering."*

King David said in Psalm 9:17, *"The wicked shall be turned into hell, and all nations that forget God."*

King Solomon, the wisest man who ever lived, (and I think it would be wise for us to listen to what the wisest man that ever lived had to say—don't you?), said these words in Proverbs 27:20: *"Hell and destruction are never full..."*

Why is hell never full? Because that great prophet Isaiah said in the book that bears his name, chapter 5:14, *"Therefore Hell hath enlarged herself, and opened her mouth without measure: and their glory, and their multitude, and their pomp, and he that rejoiceth, shall descend into it."*

As we move over into the New Testament, we find the uncompromising preacher, John the Baptist, bellowing these solemn words: *"I indeed baptize you with water unto repentance: but He that cometh after me is mightier than I, whose shoes I am not worthy to bear: he shall baptize you with the Holy Ghost, and with fire: Whose fan is in his hand, and he will throughly purge His floor, and gather his wheat into the garner; but he will burn up the chaff with UNQUENCHABLE FIRE"* (Matthew 3:11-12).

And the One of whom John spoke preached on hell. Yes, Jesus Christ preached on hell. That may come as a surprise to you because many preachers and Bible teachers today concentrate on how Jesus spoke about love, joy, and peace. And He did speak about love, joy, and peace, but, friend of mine, let it be clear that the Meek and Lowly One spoke about hell, as well as the judgment and the wrath to come. In fact, Jesus Christ preached on hell more than any other person in the Bible. Not only that, but He also preached on hell more than He did about Heaven.

Please excuse my expression, but Jesus Christ was a hell, fire, and brimstone preacher. Thank God, Jesus Christ was not like the back-scratching, ear-tickling preachers of today who use euphemisms for hell and who don't know how to temper judgment and wrath with mercy and love. Listen to these sobering words uttered by the Saviour in Matthew 5:22: *"...I say unto you, That whosoever is angry with his brother without a cause shall be in danger of the judgement: and whosoever shall say to his brother, Raca, shall be in danger of the council: but whosoever shall say, Thou fool, shall be in danger of hell fire."*

There is a clan running around the globe today telling folk that there's no hell. (I'll only give you their initials—Jehovah's Witness.) They deceive people by telling them that the word "hell" in the Bible is translated grave. When I meet up with this crowd, I kindly say to them, 'Sir or Ma'am, you can translate the word hell into anything you wish. You can translate the word hell into a double cheeseburger. You can translate the word hell into bowling alley. I'm not too concerned about how you translate the word hell. I'm more interested in how you translate the word fire. As far as I know, fire is fire, and fire burns. If, perhaps hell is a grave as you say, why do you put your deceased loved ones into a grave where there is fire? Apparently you're not smart enough to translate God's Word, so leave It be, and let God speak for Himself.'

Jesus Christ also uttered these soul-prodding words in Matthew

25:41: *"Then shall he say also unto them on the left hand, Depart from me, ye cursed, into everlasting fire, prepared for the devil and his angels..."*

You see, God did not prepare hell for people. He prepared hell for the devil and his angels, but if people act like the devil and live like the devil, they will inevitably go to hell with the devil. It's as simple as that.

Allow me to say also, that our Lord was extremely earnest about this matter of hell. He was so serious that He said these sobering words in Mark 9:47-48: *"And if thine eye offend thee, pluck it out: it is better for thee to enter into the kingdom of God with one eye, than having two eyes to be cast into hell fire: Where their worm dieth not, and the fire is not quenched."*

Jesus Christ said that it is better for one to lose a body member than to go to hell. Now that's serious.

And then John, the Great Revelator, exiled on the isle of Patmos, wrote these words in Revelation 20:15: *"And whosoever was not found written in the book of life was cast into the lake of fire."*

IS THERE A HELL? I'm afraid that that is not the appropriate question. The question is DO WE BELIEVE THAT THERE IS A HELL? Well, if you believe that the Bible is the inspired Word of God, you are compelled to believe that there is a literal burning hell.

Now, I'm not sharing anything new. You have heard about hell numerous times before. I'm just reminding you that there still is a hell, *"where their worm dieth not, and the fire is not quenched,"* and we need to believe it not only theoretically, but also practically.

WHERE IN THE WORLD IS HELL?

The second question that I am moved to ask is, *where in the world is hell?*

Let me say that we must get in our minds that not only is there a hell, but hell is a very real place. Hell is a place like America is a place. Hell is a place like Atlanta is a place. Hell is a place like your house is a place. Hell is a very real place.

So if there is a hell, and hell is a place, my question is, *where is hell?* From my studies in the Word of God, I'm of the conviction that hell is in the center of the earth. Now, you may believe that hell is in space somewhere. You may believe that hell is on Mars. Or you may be one of those dear folk who say, "I'm in hell right now" (I can assure you that you are not). The fact of the matter is that it really doesn't matter where hell is, I don't want to go there. But since hell is real, it would be safe for us to say that hell is some place. And I believe that place is the center of the earth. Here's why:

In the book of Acts 2:31, the Bible states: *"...He seeing this before spake of the resurrection of Christ, that his soul was not left in hell, neither his flesh did see corruption."*

And in Ephesians 4:9, the Bible says, *"Now that He ascended, what is it but that he also descended first into the lower parts of the earth?"*

88

And in Matthew 12:40, Jesus proclaimed these words; *"For as Jonas was three days and three nights in the whale's belly; so shall the Son of man be three nights in the heart of the earth."*

In light of these three verses, I believe that hell is in the center of this earth.

And outside of the Word of God (which, by the way, is enough), scientists tell us that about eleven miles down in the center of the earth, lie rivers of liquid fire which heat is beyond measure. Also, volcano eruptions may even testify to the fact of a burning inferno in the center of the earth.

Friend of mine, hell is a very real place! And I believe that place is in the center of this earth.

WHAT KIND OF PLACE IS HELL?

Third, I'm moved to ask the question, *what kind of place is hell?* According to the Holy Scriptures, hell is a place of sorrowful and pitiful conditions.

First of all, look with me at verse 24 of our text, Luke chapter 16: *"And he cried and said, Father Abraham, have mercy on me, and send Lazarus, that he may dip the tip of his finger in water, and cool my tongue; for I am tormented in this flame."*

In this verse, we find that **hell is a place of constant torment**. Now that word torment means continuous, painful torture. In hell there will be constant agony, constant crying, constant torment.

There are many torments in hell, but we are going to briefly take a look at three.

1. First, in hell, one will find the awful torment of unsatisfied desires. While life remains in your body, you can, in most cases, get your desires satisfied. But in hell one will desire and lust after a wet finger and never be satisfied. In hell, one will desire for a moment of rest and never be accommodated. In hell, one will lust and lust, and desire, and desire, and never be satisfied.

   Dear friend, how would you like to be in a place where you will never be able to get anything you long for?

2. Not only that, but in hell one will suffer the torment of being forever associated with the ungodly. It has often amazed me that even after severe punishment, people, generally speaking, do not change. Those of us who have visited the jails can testify to this. People who have been incarcerated for committing crimes continue to do some of these same things, even in jail. That's how it will be in hell. People who were cruel and mean on earth will be mean and cruel in hell. People who were wretched and unrepentant on earth will be unrepentant and wretched in hell. And if you're not saved you will be there with them. What an awful thought.

3. Then there will be the most familiar torment; the torment of pauseless burning. They tell me that the worst kind of pain there is, is the pain of being burned. Imagine being burned for a minute, then an hour, a day, a week, then a month, a year, FOREVER BURNING! Have you ever had a pain before? Take the worst pain that you have ever experienced and multiply it a trillion times, and you just might get a little taste of what hell is like.

Hell is an awful place! Hell is a place of constant torment. The question is, do we really believe it?

Hell is not only a place of constant torment, but my friend, hell is a place of a ceaseless annoying memory. Look with me at our text, verse 25: *"And Abraham said, SON, REMEMBER that thou in thy life time receivedst thy good things, and likewise Lazarus evil things: but now he is comforted, and thou art tormented."*

Jesus Christ reported that Abraham said to the rich man "SON, REMEMBER!" If you would allow me to use my imagination a bit. I can hear Abraham shooting these questions at the rich man: "Son, do you remember all those nights you partied and boogied all night long? Do you remember the countless number of evenings you spent with women who were not your wife, Mr. Rich Man? Do you remember? Do you remember the days you cursed Lazarus as he was at your gate begging for the crumbs that fell from your table? Do you remember the few times you went to the temple and fell asleep while Jesus was preaching the gospel that would have delivered you from your present predicament? SON, DO YOU REMEMBER?"

Memory can be an agonizing thing. There are things that I have said and done many years ago that come across my mind every now and then, and when they do, sometimes, they make my whole body flinch. I'm sure you know what I'm talking about. And every person who goes to this awful place called hell will have an agonizing and haunting memory. In hell one will remember every time he half-read a gospel tract and threw it in the trash. He will remember the face of every person who came to his door to share the gospel of Jesus Christ. In Hell he will remember every preacher he ever cursed, every blasphemous joke he ever uttered. And over and over again, he will sing the saddest song ever sung, entitled, "What Could Have Been."

HELL IS AN AWFUL PLACE! Hell is a place of an agonizing memory! The question is, DO WE BELIEVE IT?

And then according to other scripures outside of our text, we will find that hell is a place of terrifying darkness!

In Matthew 8:12, Jesus said, *"But the children of the kingdom shall be cast out into outer darkness: there shall be weeping and gnashing of teeth."*

In 2 Peter 2:4, Peter wrote: *"For if God spared not the angels that sinned, but cast them down to hell, and delivered them into chains of darkness, to be reserved unto judgment."*

Also, in 2 Peter, the Apostle wrote concerning the false prophets: *"These are wells without water, clouds that are carried with a tempest; to whom the mist of darkness is reserved for ever."*

And that great defender of the faith, Jude, called the darkness of hell: the BLACKNESS OF DARKNESS.

CHAINS OF DARKNESS! MIST OF DARKNESS! BLACKNESS OF DARKNESS! What kind of darkness is this? My friend, it is a darkness that one can feel. If you are one of those fearful souls that can't go to sleep without a night light on, I beg you, please don't go to hell. Because there won't be any light there to turn on. Well, preacher, didn't you say earlier that there will be fire in hell? How then can there be fire without light? "Nothing is impossible with God." If God says there will be darkness along with the fire in hell, then Mr. Fire will cooperate with Mr. Darkness.

It's as simple as that.

HELL IS AN AWFUL PLACE! Hell is a place of utter darkness! Do we believe it?

Also, back in our text we find that hell is such an appalling place that those in hell do not wish to see their loved ones there. Listen to Mr. Rich man: *"Then he said, I pray thee therefore, father, that thou wouldest send him to my father's house: For I have five brethren; that he may testify unto them, lest they also come into this place of torment."*

My friend, that is a miserable place where no one at all is ever welcome. That must be a terrible place where one doesn't even want to see his own family go there. But hell will do that to you. If you die and go to this awful place, you will never want to see your dear mother there. You will never want to see your Father there. You'll never want to see your brother there. You'll never want to see your loved ones there. Hell is such a dreadful place that you won't even want to see your worst enemy there. HELL IS AN AWFUL PLACE! Hell is a place where no one is welcome. But do we believe it?

And then lastly, I must say that according to God's word, hell is a place of no return. I saved this aspect of hell for last, because, to me, this has got to be the saddest part of hell. Look at what Abraham told the rich man in verse 26 of our text: *"And beside all this, between us and you there is a great gulf fixed: so that they which would pass from hence to you cannot; neither can they pass to us, that would come from hence."*

Once a person enters the gates of hell, there will be no return. There will be no second chance. There is no more hope. No more grace.

No more mercy. No more gospel. No more preachers. And yes, no more God. Once a person, is in hell, he will be locked in forever. And to me that has got to be the most horrifying aspect of hell.

Hell! the prison house of despair,
Here are some things that won't be there:
No flowers will bloom on the banks of hell;
No beauties of nature we love so well;
No comforts of home, music and song;
No friendship or joy will be found in that throng
No love, nor peace, nor one ray of light;
No blood-washed soul with face beaming bright;
No loving smile in that region of night;
No mercy, no pity, pardon nor grace;
No water; Oh God, what a terrible place!
The pangs of the lost no human can tell;
Not one moment's peace—there is no rest in hell.

HELL! the prison house of despair;
Here are some things that will be there:
Fire and brimstone are there we know;
For God in his word hath told us so:
Memory, Remorse, Suffering and Pain;
Weeping and wailing, but all in vain:
Blasphemers, swearers, haters of God,
Christ-rejectors while here on earth trod;
Murderers, gamblers, drunkards and liars
Will have their part in the lake of fire;
The filthy, the vile, the cruel and mean;
What a horrible mob in hell will be seen!
Yes, more than humans on earth can tell,
Are torments and woes of eternal Hell!
                                        —Author Unknown

HELL IS AN AWFUL PLACE! HELL IS A PLACE OF NO RETURN! The question remains, do we, as Christians, believe it?

If so, there ought to be a difference in our lives. There are two injunctions that our Saviour gave us to follow. They are found in the book of Matthew chapter 5, verses 13-16: *"Ye are the salt of the earth: but if the salt have lost his savour, wherewith shall it be salted? It is henceforth good for nothing, but to be cast out, and to be trodden under foot of men. Ye are the light of the world. A city that is set on an hill cannot be hid. Neither do men light a candle, and put it under a bushel, but on a candlestick; and it giveth light unto all that are in the house. Let your light so shine before men, that they may see your good works, and glorify your Father which is in Heaven."*

The key word in this passage is LET. This word "let" denotes that we have the light, but it is up to us to let it shine. And there are many ways that we can keep our light from shining. We, as Christians, many times keep the light from shining because of sin, because of worldliness and indifference. What is it with you, dear Christian friend? Is there a sin in your life that you are not willing to repent of? Is it your worldly attitude and demeanor? Is it your coldness, your indifference to the things of God? What is it that is keeping your light from shining? Whatever it is, you need to get it right with the Lord, because people are watching us and we need to be in a position to help "pull them out of the fire." If we believe there is a hell like we say we do, we as Christians need to live like there is a hell.

And then, in light of the fact of the reality of hell, there is something else our Lord wants us to do and that is found in Matthew 28:19-24: *"Go ye therefore, and teach all nations, baptizing them in the name of the Father, and of the Son, and of the Holy*

Ghost: Teaching them to observe all things whatsoever I have commanded you: and, lo, I am with you alway, even unto the end of the world. Amen."

I know that this is not anything profound. I know that this is nothing new. But this is what we need to hear. It is a shame that we get so familiar with the Word of God, that we don't even obey it anymore. In light of the awful fact of Hell, you and I ought to get back to the old fashion business of soul-winning. Because whether we can conceive it in our finite minds or not, those who die without Jesus Christ will spend eternity in a place *"where the worm dieth not, and the fire is not quenched."*

My friend, if perhaps you're not saved from this awful place called hell, I urge you to get saved this very moment.

Here's how: First acknowledge the fact that you are a sinner and that you're helpless to save yourself. *"For all have sinned and come short of the glory of God"* (Romans 3:23).

Second, realize that because of your sins and lost condition, there is a terrible penalty to pay, and that is eternal separation from God in hell. And then you need to recognize the fact that God loves you more than you love yourself. He loves you so much that He paid the supreme sacrifice to save you from that place by sending His only begotten Son, Jesus Christ to die for you.

"FOR GOD SO LOVED THE WORLD THAT HE GAVE HIS ONLY BEGOTTEN SON THAT WHOSOEVER BELIEVETH IN HIM SHOULD NOT PERISH, BUT HAVE EVERLASTING LIFE" (St. John 3:16).

And all you have to do in this world to have this everlasting life is simply believe in your heart that Jesus Christ died for you, was buried and was raised again by the Power of God. Then call on His name to save you. And believe me–He will.

"That if thou shalt confess with thy mouth the Lord Jesus, and shalt believe in thine heart that God hath raised Him from the dead, thou shalt be saved. For whosoever shall call upon the name of the Lord shall be saved" (Romans 10:9, 13).

APPENDIX OR
OTHER SIGNIFICANT STUFF

1. **On "Being Saved" in Black America**
   Daniel Whyte III

2. **Things You Ought to do After You Enter Through the Door**
   Daniel Whyte III

3. **Preaching Versus Pastoring**
   Pastor Louis Baldwin

4. **In Search of a Black Saviour**
   Dr. William Banks

ON "BEING SAVED"

Daniel Whyte III

While growing up in a very religious and church-going family, I often heard the phrase "Being Saved." Now to me and my peers, "Being Saved" was a rather spooky and mystical thing, and only the real holy folk could be such — whatever it was. I was under the impression that anyone who went up and took the chair after the preacher said, "The do-o-o-rs of the church are open," was saved. And then, if a person got baptized he got a little more saved. And then, if they really got a dose of this "Being Saved" stuff, they would follow a set of rules like not drinking and smoking. And these really saved folk would also engage in shouting and/or speaking in some unknown tongue on Sunday mornings. Now if a person was considered a hard case, he would have to be put on the mourner's bench until he saw a vision or felt some kind of a change. Then, he was considered saved.

Even though I was raised in this religious environment, I was still rather doubtful about this thing called "Being Saved." I just could not buy what people said "Being Saved" was. I always had questions in my mind about this matter such as: Saved from what? Saved to what? Was a person saved to live a sinless life? Could a person ever lose this savedness? If so, how and at what point? It wasn't until I was a grown man and in the Air Force that these questions, along with a host of others were answered. I finally found out what it really meant to be saved according to the Holy Scriptures. Allow me to share with you what "Being Saved" really means. But first, let me share with you what it does not mean.

WHAT "BEING SAVED" DOES NOT MEAN

I am a firm believer that before a person can fully grasp and appreciate truth, error must be exposed for what it is: error. Here are some things many believe "Being Saved" is, but is not.

1. **Having your name on a church roll does not mean that you are saved.** A person may be a good standing and long standing member of a very fine church. He may attend that church faithfully. But if he hasn't been saved, he will go to Hell with the vilest of sinners. For the Bible states in Ephesians 2:8-9: *"For by grace are ye saved through faith; and that not of yourselves: it is the gift of God: not of works, lest any man should boast."*

2. **Being baptized will not save you.** There are many baptized people in Hell. I was baptized at the age of twelve, but I didn't get saved until I was nineteen. Baptism is a very important aspect of the Christian's life, but one should only get baptized after one has been saved. This is to testify to others that you are identifying with Jesus Christ and His death, burial and resurrection. The penitent thief on the cross was saved, but he never got baptized before he died. The Apostle Paul told some Corinthian believers this in I Corinthians 1:17: *"For Christ sent me not to baptize, but to preach the gospel. Not with wisdom of words, lest the cross of Christ should be made of none effect."* Brother Paul would not have made that statement if baptism was necessary for "Being Saved."

3. **Being able to speak in an unknown tongue does not prove that one is saved.** Speaking in tongues is not evidence of being saved. In I Corinthians chapter 12, Paul asked

some rhetorical questions regarding the gifts of the Spirit that demanded some very obvious answers: *"Are all apostles? Are all prophets? Are all teachers? Are all workers of miracles? Have all the gifts of healing? Do all speak with tongues? Do all interpret?"* The obvious answer to these questions is an emphatic NO! If everyone does not have the gift of tongues, it stands to reason that tongues are not necessary to be saved.

4. **Trying to keep the law, much religious activity, and keeping the Golden Rule will not save you.** One can't keep the law because all have broken the law at some point in their lives. For the Bible states in Romans 3:23: *"For all have sinned and come short of the glory of God."* One may be a preacher, a deacon, an usher and still not be saved. One could shout, dance, sing in the choir, work on every auxiliary in the church and still die and go to Hell. Why? Because religious activity, no matter how much, no matter how sincere, does not save a soul. For the Bible says in Titus 3:5: *"Not by works of righteousness which we have done, but according to his mercy he saved us, by the washing of regeneration, and renewing of the Holy Ghost."*

5. **Seeing a vision or feeling a change at some time in your life is not a basis for "Being Saved."** True salvation is not based on sight or emotions, but rather on the eternal, infallible Word of God: the Bible. Now the Holy Scriptures state in the book of II Corinthians and Hebrews respectively that *"We walk by faith and not by sight..."* and *"Now faith is the substance of things hoped for, the evidence of things not seen."*

6. **To be born into a religious family does not assure that you are saved.** Just because your grandparents and parents

are saved or religious does not mean that you are automatically saved yourself. It is a fearful truth that every man will have to stand before the Judge of the universe for himself. Psalm 49:7 states: *"None of them can by any means redeem his brother, nor give to God a ransom for him..."*

In short, none of the above are ways of "Being Saved." There is only one way of being saved. Allow me to share it with you now.

WHAT "BEING SAVED" REALLY MEANS

Error being exposed, truth can glisten like a beautiful diamond on the backdrop of black velvet. In order for one to be truly saved, one must first:

1. **Recognize the fact that he needs to be saved. Or realize that he is a sinner and totally unable to save himself**. Let's face a cold, hard fact. We all have sinned. We all have done something wrong in our lifetime. Everyone born into this world since Adam, with the exception of Jesus Christ, has transgressed the Word of God. The Bible states in Ecclesiastes 7:20: *"There is not a just man upon earth that doeth good and sinneth not."* And the Bible also says in Romans 3:23: *"For all have sinned, and come short of the glory of God."*

2. **Second, one must realize the fact that there is a horrible punishment for those not saved**. That penalty, that punishment, is a place called Hell. Hell is as real as the house you live in, the clothes you wear, the water you drink. Now, whether you believe that there is a Hell or not, it really doesn't matter because your unbelief will not change the fact that there is a Hell. For the Bible says, *"Let God be true and every man*

a liar." If you would investigate the Holy Scriptures, you would find a myriad of verses regarding that awful place. For example, King David said in Psalm 9:17: *"The wicked shall be turned into hell and all nations that forget God."* Jesus Christ said in Matthew 5:22b: *"...Whosoever shall say thou fool shall be in danger of hell fire."* He also stated in Matthew 25:41: *"Then shall he say unto them on the left hand, depart from me ye cursed into everlasting fire prepared for the devil and his angels."* So, friend of mine, there is a very severe punishment for the unsaved and their sins. And that is a place called HELL.

3. The third thing that we must recognize is that God loves us very, very much. *"God is not willing that any man should perish"* (II Peter 3:9). God loves us so much that He gave His only Son. As the Bible states: *"...God so loved the world that he gave his only begotten Son, that whosoever believeth in him should not perish, but have everlasting life"* (John 3:16). Someone once said, "That if anybody ought to want to go to Heaven, it ought to be black folk with all the trouble we've seen." So if it is our desire to bypass that awful place called Hell (and it should be), we need to realize that God loves us more than we love ourselves. And He has made a way for us to escape. And that is by simply believing in the person and accomplished work of Jesus Christ, plus nothing, minus nothing. Now the way for us to apply this to our own lives is to be willing to repent (that is to change our minds about sin), and do as Romans 10: 9-13 says: to simply believe with your heart that Jesus Christ died, was buried and rose again for your sins, and then call upon the Lord in prayer and ask Him to save your soul. And believe me, He will. Romans 10: 9-13: *"That if thou shalt confess with thy mouth the Lord Jesus, and shalt believe in thine heart that God hath raised him from the dead, thou shalt be saved. For whosoever shall call upon the name of the Lord shall be saved."*

THINGS YOU OUGHT TO DO AFTER YOU ENTER THROUGH THE DOOR

Daniel Whyte III

Dear Friend, this article is primarily for people who have already entered through the "Door" of Life by accepting Jesus Christ as their Saviour. If you have not accepted Jesus Christ as your personal Saviour as of yet, please do so today by simply believing in Jesus Christ — that He died for you, that He was buried and rose again — and by calling on His Name to save you: *"For whosoever shall call upon the name of the Lord shall be saved"* (Romans 10:13).

Jesus Christ said, *"I am the door: by me if any man enter in, he shall be saved, and shall go in and out and find pasture"* (John 10:9).

I am convinced that there are many people who have entered through the "Door," that is, they have been truly saved, but, sadly, no one ever sat down with them and told them correctly what they should do after they have entered through the "Door."

Getting saved is most important, but what you do after you are saved is very important as well. Following are seven things that you definitely need to do after you are saved:

1. Get Baptized. Matthew 28:19: *"Go ye therefore, and teach all nations, baptizing them in the name of the Father, and of the Son, and of the Holy Ghost."* It is very important that you obey the Lord and follow Him in Believers' Baptism. Even if you were baptized at another time in your life, if you are just now truly getting saved, you still need to be baptized again because you were not saved the first time you were baptized. You see, we don't get baptized to be saved; rather, we get baptized because we are saved.

2. Join with a good church. Hebrews 10:25: *"Not forsaking the assembling of ourselves together, as the manner of some is; but exhorting one another: and so much the more, as ye see the day approaching."* Let's face it: everything that says church on it is not necessarily a church of the Lord Jesus Christ. For there are many false churches and teachers in the world. Below are some marks of a good church:

A. The pastor preaches from the Word of God — the Bible — and he strives to practice what he preaches.

B. The church stands on the basics of the Christian faith. The basics of the Christian faith are:

- The Bible is inspired by God
- The Deity of Jesus Christ
- The Blood Atonement for sin by Jesus Christ
- Salvation by Faith in Jesus Christ
- The imminent Return of Jesus Christ

C. An emphasis is placed on reaching out to others with the gospel of Jesus Christ.

D. The love of Jesus Christ is shown.

These are just a few marks of a good church. Pray and follow the Lord's leading.

3. Allow yourself to be trained. Matthew 28:20:

"Teaching them to observe all things whatsoever I have commanded you: and, lo, I am with you alway, even unto the end of the world. Amen." This will mean that you will have to humble yourself and listen to your pastor and those he appoints to help you. You see, becoming a Christian is something totally new to you and there are many important things that you will have to learn from others who are trained and have the experience.

4. Pray daily. Luke 18:1: *"And he spake a parable unto them to this end, that men ought always to pray and not to faint."* You will find that regular prayer unto God will be one of your greatest sources of strength, power and blessing.

5. Read your Bible daily. Romans 10:17: *"So then faith cometh by hearing, and hearing by the word of God."* As they say, "When you pray, you talk to God. When you read your Bible, God talks to you." Do you want to live a vibrant, strong, useful and successful Christian life? Then you will want to read and meditate on your Bible daily.

6. Witness for Christ daily. Acts 1:8: *"But ye shall receive power, after that the Holy Ghost is come upon you: and ye shall be witnesses unto me both in Jerusalem, and in all Judea, and in Samaria, and unto the uttermost part of the earth."* Jesus Christ commands us to witness for Him. One of the greatest joys you will ever have in this life is to share the Gospel of Jesus Christ with another person. A greater joy is to see them come to know your Saviour as their Saviour. So plant the seed everywhere you go and allow God to use you to *"turn many from darkness to light."*

7. If you are willing to follow Jesus Christ as one of His disciples, pray with me the following prayer: *Holy*

Father, I pray in the name of Jesus Christ please forgive and cleanse me of all sin. Create within me a pure heart and a right spirit. Please help me to do the things that I just read, and grant me your grace to be a Christian that will glorify your name. In the name of Jesus Christ I pray. Amen.

Congratulations on entering through the "Door" of Eternal Life by believing in our Lord and Saviour Jesus Christ. Trusting Jesus Christ as your personal Saviour is the most important thing you will ever do. Now that you are saved, let's live for the One who died for us. God bless you as you serve Him.

PREACHING VERSUS PASTORING

Rev. Louis Baldwin

Rev. Louis Baldwin is pastor of the Crossroads Baptist Church in Bailey's Crossroads, Virginia

Over the years, as the pastor of the Crossroads Baptist Church, I have been addressed as Reverend, Preacher, Pastor, and a few other titles. The title that I'm addressed most often by my people is "Pastor." I thank the Lord that I'm a preacher of the Word of God. God did not just call me to be a "Preacher of the Word of God," but a "Pastor of the Church of God." I'm afraid today that we're producing lots of preachers but very few real pastors. A preacher often preaches to or at people; a real pastor shepherds people. With such a great need in the black community to establish Bible-believing Baptist Churches, we need to stop preaching at people, and start pastoring people (this always includes preaching the Word of God).

The Apostle Peter tells us in I Peter 5:2-3: *"Feed the flock of God which is among you, taking the oversight thereof, not by constraint, but willingly; not for filthy lucre, but of a ready mind; neither as being lords over God's heritage, but being ensamples to the flock."* The Word of God tells me as a pastor that the flock is *"God's heritage"* and He has given me the awesome responsibility of being an under-shepherd of the "Chief Shepherd" of His flock.

As I read the Word of God and strive to pastor my flock, I find that Peter exhorts us to do three important things as pastors.

First, a pastor must **lead his people.** The Word of God says,

111

"taking the oversight thereof." A church is not a corporation that you can demand things of your employees. It is a body of believers that you must lead in the direction it needs to go. Black people today are looking for leadership that is competent and faithful. There are many changes that need to occur among our people if we are to establish New Testament churches among them.

So often, I see our young black preachers coming out of school trying to pound people to change. A pastor learns how to lead people to change. Real pastoral leadership can accomplish this without ever compromising the Word of God. Good leadership is not something that you are born with, but something that is learned.

Second, a pastor must *love his people*. There is nothing more disgusting to me than to hear pastors criticizing, condemning, and complaining about their people. Next to the Lord, and my family, I love my flock. God has given them to me. They are not perfect, and neither am I. Learn to love your people even if you haven't taught them to take care of you. Peter says, *"not by constraint, but willingly; not for filthy lucre, but of a ready mind."* A pastor is not one who just serves out of obligation or a sense of duty. It is an honor to pastor a flock of people (regardless the size). Don't make your people feel as though they are blessed to have you. It is by the grace of God that He saw fit to use any of us.

A pastor loves his people by demonstrating that he doesn't pastor for personal gain. So many today look at success as having a group of quality people, who are financially able to take care of the preacher. There is absolutely nothing wrong with the pastor being well provided for by his people. As a matter of fact, it is taught in the Scriptures. The Bible says, *"Even so hath the Lord ordained that they which preached the gospel should live of the gospel"* (I Corinthians 9:14).

However, using the pastorate as a means of personal gain is an attitude that is forbidden in the Scriptures. A pastor should always be enthusiastic about the ministry, not the money. A preacher is a pastor when he loves the people that God has given him to shepherd.

Third, a pastor is one who *lives by example before his people*. The Apostle Peter exhorts us to be a model for our people, *"Neither as being lords over God's heritage, but being ensamples to the flock."* The old saying, "Do as I say, and not as I do" is inappropriate for the ministry. I have always begged God to help me to "practice what I preach." One of the greatest qualities a pastor can have is to be a good example to his flock. Don't preach witnessing if you don't witness. Don't preach holiness if you don't live holy. Don't preach on the family if you don't lead your family. Don't preach on giving if you don't give. A real pastor does not *tell* his people what to do without being willing to *show* them what to do.

Across the country, I have heard many outstanding black preachers. Preachers don't build churches, pastors and evangelist-missionaries build churches. If we are going to see churches established to reach our people, we need to see more of our great preachers become pastors. I wonder today, as you examine your ministry, are you *preaching* or *pastoring*. It does make a difference to your people!

IN SEARCH OF A BLACK SAVIOUR

Dr. William Banks

Dr. Banks has faithfully pastored several churches down through the years. He is also a former professor at Moody Bible Institute in Chicago, Illinois, and is a renown author and conference speaker.

Men who search the Bible for race identification often quote Job 30:30: *"My skin is black upon me..."* Or Jeremiah 8:21: *"I am black..."* However, neither Job nor Jeremiah dealt with skin color as a racial characteristic. Both spoke of despair, dismay, and disappointment. They had the "blacks." Today we have the "blues."

The search for race identification has led others to John's description of Christ in the Book of Revelation. We read in Chapter One, Verse 14: *"His head and his hair were white like wool..."* That wooly head and hair means Christ was a black man, right?

No. Not necessarily. *"White like wool"* emphasizes color, not material. And white hair signifies old age and wisdom. John wanted to show that the Lord Jesus Christ, holy and all-wise, was none other that the *"Ancient of Days"* (Daniel 7:9, 13, 22).

The point is this: We have no proof of evidence that Jesus Christ was a black Man. In fact, we don't know what color He was.

But now, for the sake of argument, suppose He was One of US. Suppose you could identify with Him racially. What difference would it make? What would you do with Him? I mean, would you then believe that He shed His blood on the cross for your sins?

Or is it that you're more interested in the SKIN issue than the SIN issue? You see, no matter what the color of our skin is, sin is in our hearts. We show our sinful nature by crime, drunkenness, hatred, murder, racism, war, etc. And the end result is death — physical death, and spiritual death, which is hell.

So, if you want to save your skin, you'd better get the sin problem straightened out. And the only one who can fix you up is Jesus Christ. He has no hang-ups about skin color and race. Indeed, He said, *"And I, if I be lifted up from the earth, I will draw all men unto me"* (John 12:32).

The Christ of the Bible—whatever His color—is able to meet the needs of black men and women, black boys and girls. So, there is no need to search the Scriptures for a black Saviour. What we need to do is accept the Saviour Who is there—Jesus Christ Who died for all men, be they black, brown, red, yellow, or white.

Believe on Him—as He is; and He will accept you—as you are.

> Hallelujah, I have found Him
> Whom my soul so long had craved!
> Jesus satisfies my longing:
> Through His blood I now am saved.

The Bible states in the book of Romans 10:9 & 13: *"That if thou shalt confess with thy mouth the Lord Jesus, and shalt believe in thine heart that God hath raised him from the dead, thou shalt be saved."*

"For whosoever shall call upon the name of the Lord shall be saved."

Now, dear friend, if you have believed in your heart that Jesus Christ died, was buried, and rose from the dead for you, and you have called upon Him, in prayer, to save you, then you are saved and I rejoice in your decision to trust Christ as Saviour.

6201426R0

Made in the USA
Lexington, KY
28 July 2010